Santa Barbara
Mountain Bikes

Santa Barbara Outdoor Companion Series

McNally & Loftin Publications by
Raymond Ford, Jr.

Day Hikes of the Santa Barbara Foothills (1984)
Santa Barbara Wildfires (1990)
Santa Barbara Mountain Bikes (1992)
Santa Barbara Recreational Map Series
  Map # 1   San Rafael Wilderness
        2   Santa Barbara Front Country Hikes
        3   Dick Smith Wilderness
        4   Santa Barbara Mountain Bike Routes
        5   Figueroa Mountain Hiking and Biking
        6   Santa Ynez Valley Road Bicycling

Santa Barbara
Mountain Bikes

Raymond Ford, Jr.

Copyright © Raymond Ford, Jr. 1992
McNally & Loftin, Publishers
5390 Overpass Road,
Santa Barbara, CA 93111

Printed and Bound by
Kimberly Press, Inc.
Goleta, CA

Illustrations are by Julie Kummel
Photographs by Ray Ford. Cover Photo: Little Pine Mountain;
Rear Cover: Gibraltar Trail near the mouth of Mono Creek; Title
Page: Agua Caliente Canyon above the dam.
Chumash figures, maps and chapters designed by Ray Ford using a
Macintosh IIsi. Pagemaker was used for page design, and Freehand
for maps and drawings. The typestyle is New Century Schoolbook.

LIBRARY OF CONGRESS CATALOGING-IN-PUBLICATION DATA

Ford, Raymond, 1943—
    Santa Barbara mountain bikes / Raymond Ford, Jr.
        p.   cm.
    ISBN 0—87461—105—9: $9.95
    1. All terrain cycling—California—Santa Barbara County—
    —Guidebooks. 2. Sannta Barbara County (Calif)—Guidebooks.
    GV1045.5.C2F67   1992
    796.6'4'0979491—dc20   92-11631
                                                        CIP

McNally & Loftin, Publisher

In memory of Terry Gearhart
1949-1987

"In mountain biking, the background chattering of the mind is silenced; life becomes the passage, not the destination."
Hank Barlow

Table of Contents

Introduction

Mountain Pedals 1

Mountain Bike Controversies 13

A Code of Ethics 27

Wilderness & Mountain Bikes 31

 # Introduction

For many of us who get out into the back country as often as we can, a mountain bike is the vehicle that allows us the opportunity to re-acquaint ourselves with nature and to re-establish a relationship that seems to get blasted to hell and back in the city.

A mountain bike makes it possible to explore a much wider area of the Forest than is often possible on foot. There are incredible places to see and to experience here—hidden sandstone narrows, deep pools, hot springs, high country filled with pine forests, wild places that defy description. A mountain bike is a means to these places and experiences.

Because of its link to technology and the potential for abuse, mountain biking is under attack from some environmental groups—notably the Sierra Club—which is dedicated to the proposition that no trail should be violated by the fat track of a mountain bike. Some would say that you don't see anything on a mountain bike. You are going too fast. Not true. Hiking is not the only way to experience nature.

There is an indefinable dimension to mountain biking. "In mountain biking, the background chattering of the mind is silenced," Hank Barlow writes. "Life becomes the passage, not the destination."

Sometimes I think we are too caught up in detail. We see things while ignoring the form, the essence of which things are made. To experience nature fully is to integrate—sounds, smells, textures, soft shadings, intricate patterns, and delicate emotions. It is to learn patience, practice humility, express joy, and to share it with others.

The vehicle is the means, not the end; to experience, not just see, the goal—a "celebration of living" is what Barlow calls it—a zest for life and a relationship with it that transcends the vehicle.

But if used carelessly, a mountain bike can damage and destroy—both the natural resource and other people's experiences. If this should occur, there is no guarantee that mountain bikers will continue to be allowed to use trails in the Santa Barbara area.

There is no long standing tradition of mountain bike use on trails or jeep roads in either the Front Country or the Back Country. To be accepted as a legitimate part of the trail user community, they must be used with sensitivity and care.

This is especially true along the Santa Barbara Front Country, where thousands of hikers use the trails each year. Thus far, most hikers seem willing to accept mountain bikes on Front Country trails, but patience with those bicyclists who either ride too fast or cause environmental damage is wearing thin.

A letter I received from a fellow trail user regarding mountain bikes on Jesusita Trail expresses the frustration that many hikers and horse riders have. He writes:

"The switchbacks have been especially damaged. There is not one water bar left. They have been pounded out of existence. In a number of places the trail resembles a ditch....

"As we were going up the trail, a biker came down at an excessive speed, but luckily saw us in time to slow down, otherwise, it could have been a disaster. When the Forest Service held its hearings, I was one of those trail users that consented to giving the mountain bike people a chance to use the trails, to see how things would work out.

"Now, after seeing how damaging mountain bikers are to trails, plus the danger they pose when speeding, I am convinced that they are incompatible with trails.

"Unless there is a real change in how some—even if they are only a few—use the trails, perhaps it is time to ban them from the Front Country."

The feelings expressed in this letter have been echoed as well by Forest Service officials. Pat Pontes, the head ranger for the Santa Barbara Ranger District, which oversees Front Country trail use, has also become concerned about irresponsible mountain bike use on these trails.

"I am writing a personal note to alert you to a developing problem that exists on the Santa Barbara Front forest trail system," he said. "Some bicyclists are riding downhill at an excessive speed! Your continued use of these trails is in jeopardy.

"During the last few months we have found some groups of bicyclists are riding down hill on the trails and up on the bank's edge/slope above the trail tread. This is causing an eyebrow effect, and soil is eroding onto the trail. Also the braking action of fast riders is causing mechanical erosion in the tread (a U-shaped depression) that is difficult to water bar. Some individuals are beginning to cut switchbacks, locking their brakes downward to the trail below. This severely damages the trail by causing accelerated soil erosion and water channeling....

"I am concerned that we are close to meeting the criteria for bicycle regulation on some trails."

Mountain bikes provide a wonderful way to experience the out-of-doors. It is difficult for to me describe just what it means to ride out in the back country. Perhaps it is as simple as the circular rhythm of my pedals moving up and down as I pass through the country, seeing not only the detail of the land but its grace and form, a beauty that I find in its wholeness. Simply put, it is an important part of my life.

Unless we are all careful about how we ride, however, this is a pleasure that we might not always enjoy. Please ride carefully as you go through the countryside. Enjoy it to its fullest. But take care not to destroy either the land or the rights of other trail users to experience it in their own way.

 # Mountain Pedals

With the midday harshness on the mountainsides softened by alpenglow, the back country reaches out like a promise, serrated silhouettes of ridgeline, like riders on a purple haze. Sitting astride my mountain bike I breathe quietly from my perch atop the Sierra Madre Mountains, absorbing the moods and the sounds, the delicate interplay of breeze and bird song, just having begun a three-day ride that leads through the heart of this country.

I look across ranges of chaparral, ninety percent of which is covered by a thin blanket of this plant community. But these mountains, like the front country, also have their own charm—albeit a little more difficult to reach—but that is what makes the Santa Barbara back country one of the best and most challenging mountain bike areas in Southern California.

The challenges aren't ones always to be found out on the trail. Not everyone (including most members of the Sierra Club) thinks that mountain bikes belong in the backcountry. Standing here, I can understand their concerns. This is country that has a feeling of raw power, a primitive country that has survived intact mainly due to an inherent toughness, a wildness that man has been unable to subdue. Loving it, they want to protect it, a motivation that I understand completely.

"Trails are made for feet, roads for wheels," my good friend Bob Easton, an ardent conservationist and community leader who has helped establish most of Santa Barbara's environmental organizations, explains over and over to me. "Bikes just don't belong in the backcountry."

But I wonder. Is there a right way to explore this land? Can you only get in touch with it on foot? What the backcountry suggests to me is freedom, the freedom to get away from the heavy-handed restrictions and pressures of civilization for a few moments or days, to slow my pace down and get back in tune with nature's harmonies.

The Santa Barbara backcountry is not only a place to learn about, but to learn from—hard lessons, like those discovered by pioneer settlers who tried to make a go of it near the confluence of Manzana Creek and the Sisquoc River. Aesthetic lessons as well—about the beauty that can be found if you look deeply. Perhaps most of all, lessons about values—learning about nature's needs as well as one's own, and how to live in a way so that both are nurtured.

The steady pace of my mountain pedals moving up and down in circular rhythm seems to me equally as harmonious as footsteps. There is not only the detail of the land to be appreciated but its grace and its form—a beauty to be found in its wholeness. The true power of a wildflower, I think, isn't in what we know about it, or whether we can name it or not, but in the way it reaches out to us, in the process creating an emotional bond that draws us close to the land.

I remember a time listening to Bob Easton telling me about a trip of his to this area in the 1930s. "All of a sudden I got to one place on the trail," Bob explained to me, "and I thought I could hear them—the footsteps of the Chumash just ahead of me, out of sight, around the corner. They were soft steps, the steps of a people who had found a oneness with the land."

We have lost that ability, to walk softly on the earth. But I wonder if it need be re-discovered solely by foot.

The Sierra Madre Mountains

It is a land that I visit often, both on foot and on bike. It is early May, a good time to be riding here, and the pastel coloring of spring has blurred the harshness.

Though technically spring begins in December or January with the onset of the rainy season, late March through early

May is the period of greatest transformation. Grassy meadows turn a deep, rich shade of green, wildflowers make the mountains magically colorful, and for at least two months of the year this becomes a promised land, a land easy to fall in love with.

The evening's destination is Painted Rock Campground, 12 miles east along the crest of the Sierra Madre Mountains. After the strenuous uphill effort getting to the top of the mountain, the ride across is both easy and soothing, with rolling hills that offer gentle climbs and mellow downhills. In the distance the dirt path curves its way around and over a series of knolls. The next half hour's ride is through small *potreros*, the Spanish word for "meadow". As the tensions and pressures begin to slip away it becomes easier and easier to be captured by the moment, by the excitement and the stimulation, and by a sense of calmness that comes from being in harmonious surroundings.

I remember the many times I have spent backpacking in these mountains, getting to know the back country intimately. It is surprising land. In the midst of the chaparral are Chumash rock art sites, pioneer homesteads, swimming holes, sandstone mazes, and secluded off-trail canyons where you can explore to your heart's content. As always, there is the aroma, air filled with resinous oils that exude a fragrance which is washed across the countryside in the breeze, a minty smell full of a richness that envelopes you.

Beyond the Cuyama Valley are the Caliente Mountains, and beyond those are the Temblors, the trembling mountains, known as such because of the San Andreas Fault runs along their entire length. There is a vastness to this panorama, room enough to get lost in, space enough to explore for a lifetime.

The high point is 6,700 foot Big Pine Mountain. Until the mid-1980s its thousand-foot cliffs were the nesting territory of a pair of California condors. If the efforts of the Condor Recovery Team are successful, one day it will be again. Much of the land between it and the third range, the Sierra Madres, is composed of two adjoining wildernesses: the 150,000-acre

View across Pine Corral to Montgomery Potrero, three square miles of meadows and spectacular sandstone outcroppings atop the Sierra Madre Mountains. Painted Rock Campground is located here.

San Rafael Wilderness; and the 75,000-acre Dick Smith Wilderness. Though mountain bikes are not allowed in either of these areas, there are still several hundred miles of dirt roads and trails open to bicycles.

Most of the trails date to the late 1800s when miners, hunters, and pioneer settlers began to swarm into the back country; the dirt roads to the 1920s and 1930s when the Forest Service began to provide access for fire protection. In combination the roads and trails offer at least 20 different day loops, varying in length from 5 to 35 miles and in difficulty from easy to quite strenuous. Many other possibilities are also available if combined with a shuttle and/or a night or more spent out bikepacking.

From the Sierra Madre Road, a thin line can be seen cutting across the flank of Big Pine. This is Buckhorn Fire Road, a 20-foot wide fire lane constructed by CCC crews in the 1930s which separates the San Rafael and Dick Smith wildernesses.

Our ride is one that might be the finest in this part of Southern California. Beginning near the small town of New Cuyama, located on the northern edge of Santa Barbara County, it encompasses the highest and most spectacular parts of the Sierra Madre and San Rafael Mountains. Due to the rugged nature of the topography there are no direct routes from Cuyama to the coast—only a maze of trails and rough jeep routes, all closed to motorized activity.

By car it is 120 miles of highway driving to Cuyama from Santa Barbara, the first 60 of those north on Highway 101 to Santa Maria; the last 60 east on Highway 166. The return route by bike is a bit shorter—55 miles. A series of switchbacks wind for eight miles up to the crest of the Sierra Madres, and from there the ride is along the crest of these mountains, across the San Rafaels, and eventually down into the Santa Ynez Valley to Upper Oso Campground.

Painted Rock
We are not too far from Painted Rock Camp, secluded in the midst of sandstone outcroppings and meadows characteristic

of the Sierra Madre Mountains. This crestline is unique in that it is not capped by chaparral for the most part, but large open expanses of potrero. Underlain by resistant sandstones, the Sierra Madres have a thin covering of Monterey Shale, soft rock that has weathered to form a relatively long, even top, with loamy clays that support a variety of grasses, and in the springtime, acres of wildflowers. The view from just above the camp is breathtaking.

The land opens up to several square miles of grassland filled with strange porpoise, dolphin, and whale-like sandstone formations. In April and May there are literally thousands upon thousands of flowers: cream cups, goldfields, poppies, lupine, and countless others. In places the landscape is not green but golden yellow; in others a soft blue or creamy white.

The wind always seems to blow here. Rippling through hundreds of acres of grass, the rhythmic swaying motion makes the land appear to be moving. Softly and gently, the wind strokes the backs of the green-tassled grasses and the lighter jade-green undersides flash briefly in the sunlight. This light green surface is what seems to move, as if separate from the rooted stalks.

In the mornings and evenings there are always cliff and violet-green swallows darting through the air, stealthily chasing clouds of winged insects that feed upon the grasses. Flitting, soaring, darting, their maneuvers are mindboggling. It is the sandstone shapes, however, which give character and meaning to this place. The bedrock has been upthrust and throughout the meadow thin edges of it have surfaced, tan fins of rock, like prehistoric sea creatures cavorting in the sea of grass and wildflower.

I stay for several minutes more, absorbing the magical quality of this place. Below me the riders swoop back and forth, darting swallow-like down the grassy switchbacks to camp. Then I head down myself, back and forth, the feeling of the wind and motion making me feel that I, too, am like grass being blown across the land. In this feeling of motion—of flowing with the land and time—is much of what mountain

Mountain bikers enjoy the view out over Lion Canyon from the Sierra Madre Ridge Road. Cuyama Valley is in the distance.

After 2 days of riding across the Sierra Madres, a reward awaits this rider—the beautiful pine forests atop 6700' Big Pine Mountain.

biking means to me. It is a feeling extremely important to many mountain bikers, and one not easily described to those hikers who want to ban bicycles from this country.

The camp is picturesque, a single table and fire pit beneath a large canopy-shaped oak tree. There is a horse corral, and even an outhouse. A small cave is situated nearby, 30 feet above the ground.

Womb-like, this cave is shaped like the interior of a large eggshell, eight feet deep and across, perhaps six feet in height. On the walls, near the back, are small paintings done in reds and charcoal blacks, on the ceiling a two-foot diameter sun, its rays radiating outward in all directions. There is just enough room inside to sit back quietly against the curved walls and absorb the mood.

This is a place of calm, a power spot, a centering place. The rock is cool, and though the evening wind has picked up and is blowing misty clouds of fog up the mountainside, our sanctuary is seemingly unaffected by the world outside. I spend as many moments as I can in wind-sculptured caves such as this, contemplating the rock art, making friends with the evening wind, feeling the rhythm of nature's circular patterns.

A Spectacular Ride

In the morning warm sunlight filters through the oak branches. For breakfast there is plenty of cowboy coffee and granola, and ample time for a hike. Afterward we review the day's activities. From our present elevation of 4,500 feet we will continue gradually uphill along the Sierra Madres for 10 miles then begin to climb more steeply up and over a 6,500 foot saddle near Big Pine Mountain. The total mileage won't be great, not more than 20 miles, but because of the ups and downs, the actual elevation gain will be close to 4,000 feet. Nor will water be available until near the day's end, forcing us to depend on what we take with us from camp.

Filling water bottles and making a second check to see that we have left the camp in better condition than we found it, we are on our way. A mile beyond Montgomery Potrero is a second meadow, Pine Corral Potrero, and in between an immense canyon composed almost entirely of sandstone called Lion Canyon. We spend two hours exploring its depths: at one point we find ourselves following black bear tracks into the arroyo; at another those of a medium-sized mountain lion. Both impart a sense of power and mystery to the canyon.

The next few hours we ride through a series of other potreros, then begin to ascend into the San Rafael Mountains. The overwhelming feeling is that of motion, of moving with and being part of the land. On the uphills I develop an easy pedaling rhythm—what I call my "all day pace". On the downhills I coast, a carefree submission to the effects of gravity, though softly tempered by a light tapping of my brakes. Gradually the vegetation begins to change as we leave the grasses behind and encounter scattered pinyon pines and juniper, then small stands of big cone spruce, a close relative of the Douglas fir, on the shaded north slopes.

As the road steepens there are increasing numbers of conifers, and a new smell, that of the pine forest. It is hot, but at this altitude the breeze takes the edge off it, and just before a particularly steep section, we come to a small water source called Chokecherry Springs, thankfully, because we are near the end of our water.

We arrive several hours later at Big Pine Camp, surrounded by thick forests of ponderosa and sugar pines, incense cedar, and spruce. Riding for the last 5 miles has been a revelation. In viewing this area from the Santa Ynez Mountains it is difficult to believe such forests exist. But that again is the surprising nature of the Santa Barbara backcountry.

Evening Camp

Because the camp is actually several hundred yards inside the San Rafael Wilderness we leave our bikes hidden along the road and pack in our gear. Before dinner we hike to the top of Big Pine, at 6,762' feet the highest point in the County. The chaparral is stunted at this elevation, and the understory is open and littered with thick beds of pine needles, making movement easy. After the day's effort we sit back against large ponderosa pines and enjoy what might be the finest views available from anywhere in the County: snow-covered Sierras on the northern horizon; Santa Cruz Island, the largest of the Channel Islands, to the south; and mountainous ranges and deep canyons in all other directions. Have we really only been gone since yesterday?

We have another relaxing evening by the fire, listening to the crackle of flames and other night sounds, sharing and re-sharing moments accumulated from the day's activities. In the dark star-filled sky the tall silhouetted tree forms sway in the night breeze, which makes a soft sound as it rustles through the pine needles. Other than that there is total silence—no birds, no planes, no stream, nothing save the flicker of flame. The need for sleep catches up with us finally and after a few minutes of feeble resistance we all turn in.

In the morning we rise lazily, not wanting to be on our way, nor wanting the day or the trip to end. The air warms slowly in the shadows of the forest and we extend the morning fire until near leaving time before quenching it completely. From here it is 27 miles back down to the Santa Ynez Valley, most of it is downhill so we do not need to rush.

During those last few hours I try to define exactly what has been so precious about this trip, as well as the Santa Barbara backcountry. Nothing tangible, I think. Just a sense of goodness—a *wellness* that pervades my body and that carries me over the crest of the Santa Ynez Mountains and back into town.

A poem by Cynthia Miller expresses much of the feeling that I, and I'm sure others, have for mountain biking:

> *Every Day that summer*
> *from my mountain cabin*
> *I pedalled and pushed*
> *over rocky trails, around*

old mines, rotted timbers,
exhausted dreams.
    Every day
my yellow Cannondale and I
feeling my muscles stronger
my heart pounding smoother
my gloved hands gripping balance
between the brakes—between gravity
and courage.
    Every day
my machine and I tested theories
of ascent
up to intangible fences and signs
found somewhere between gravity,
strength and time.
    Every day
finding new skills and trails
while learning no one has courage—
we merely use it
whenever it appears.
    Every day
I rode those mountains
with their steep descents
and my constant need to explore—
searching,
    every day
wanting nothing more than that place
in the mind where there's no
difference in attention
between riding
    and where it leads.

 # Mountain Bike Controversies

I don't think that anybody at Specialized Bicycle realized what the impact would be when they introduced the first production mountain bike, the *Stumpjumper*, in the early 1980s. Prior to this time mountain bikes were known as "clunkers," an odd assortment of road bike, motorcycle, and home-jerried parts attached to a one-speed Schwinn bike frame.

I built my first one in 1980. It was only a 5 speed, far too heavy, had a rear drum brake that didn't work when it got wet, and the frame didn't fit my 6' 2" build very well. Worst of all, putting the assorted parts together was expensive. But I loved it. For the first time I could ride up to Little Pine or across West Camino Cielo or beyond Gibraltar Dam. I was in heaven.

Then I got my first Stumpjumper. It cost $500—an unheard of sum for a bike then—and the angles were pretty relaxed, meaning that it didn't climb hills very well (but way better than my clunker). But, boy, could you cruise on it. In 1983 I completed my first overnight trip through the backcountry—the ride across the Sierra Madre Mountains described earlier. From then on this became an annual trip (and still is).

A Controversy Develops

By the mid-80s mountain bikes had surpassed road bikes in sales, and more and more people were starting to ride them in the backcountry. By 1985, more than a half million of them had been sold.

What about the impact on wilderness areas? This was one of the first questions that many hikers asked about the rapidly growing popularity of mountain biking. Hard-fought political battles had been waged in Congress to protect the non-mechanized, non-motorized status of wilderness. What, they asked, would happen to wilderness if mountain bikes were allowed in them?

At first, foresters agreed with hikers that they should be banned, since the *Code of Federal Regulation* contained a section (CRF 261.16-b) that made "possessing or using a hang glider or bicycle" illegal. Later this was amended to read "Possessing or using a bicycle, wagon, cart, or other vehicle." However, in a letter to the nation's regional foresters on March 9, 1982 J.B. Hilmon, Associate Deputy Chief of the U.S. Forest Service, left the possibility of their use in wilderness areas open to negotiation

"It was our intent to provide for the prohibition of bicycles only where their presence created a conflict or problems," he told them, "and to implement the prohibition by use of an order for a specific wilderness." What this meant was that bicycle closure for each wilderness most likely would be decided on a case-by-case basis.

On June 11, 1982, a few months later, Ronald McCormick, Acting Director of Recreation for the Forest Service, reaffirmed this position in a letter sent out to each Forest Supervisor: "We can look at these types of 'vehicles' as being primitive, muscle powered, aids to transporting," he explained. "The history of wilderness exploration has shown that early users of the American frontier and wilderness relied on bicycles, carts, and other primitive wheeled devices to transport their possessions. Prohibitions of these devices should be done by issuing a special order in those cases where a conflict, problem or unacceptable resource damage is occurring."

Within the year, however, enough protest from groups such as the Sierra Club had reached Washington that in 1983 Chief Forester, Max Peterson, ordered a ban on the use or possession of bicycles in wilderness areas.

"But what about the thousands of miles of trails which lay outside designated wilderness?" hiker and equestrian groups also asked. Though yet to formulate a national policy on mountain bikes, by 1984 the Sierra Club had begun to question whether they should be allowed on any trail.

The lead article in the July-August, 1984 issue of *Condor Call*, a newspaper published by the local chapter of the Sierra Club, brought the issue out into the open for the first time. Written by Robin Ives, it was titled "Mountain Bikes Pose Backcountry Hazard".

"Will we have an all terrain bicycle section, ranging from beaches to back country lakes and peaks?" she asked. Or "Will we conclude that bicycles tear up trails excessively and constitute a hazard to pedestrian travel?"

A letter from long time Sierra Club member Dirk Woestenburg, reprinted in the article, seemed to answer which position the author felt the Club should take. "I could not help but reflect on the futility of working to maintain a trail [the San Ysidro] which was built to serve hikers, horses and pack animals and see it damaged by vehicles," he noted in frustration. "I feel it is time to take a stand before the situation becomes worse. The very nature of the bicycle, its high tread loading caused by its small cross-section tires and the tremendous speed differential between hikers and downhill bicyclists makes it a threat to both the trail and the hiker."

Forest Service Symposium

In Santa Barbara, by the spring of 1985, the issue of whether mountain bikes should be allowed on trails in such areas as the Front Country, the upper Santa Ynez River canyons, Little Pine, and Figueroa Mountain had come to a head. After receiving a series of letters from hikers and horse riders about near misses on local trails and discourteous behavior exhibited by some of the bike riders, the Forest Service recognized that a possible hazard might exist.

Rather than handing down an edict either supporting or banning bicycle use the Forest Supervisor, Fritz deHoll, challenged interested groups (hikers, equestrian, bicyclists, Sierra Club) to sit down together and work together to determine "whether a problem existed and present collectively to the Forest [Service] an alternative or solution to the problem." If a compromise could be reached, deHoll agreed that he would adopt it as Forest policy.

The first Forest Service Mountain Bike Symposium was held August 29, 1985 at Forest Service headquarters on Calle Real in Goleta, with more than fifty people in attendance. One huge question loomed in everyone's minds. Would these groups be able to work together or would the meetings quickly break down into bitter infighting?

Participants divided into small groups, their main task to develop a list of "perceptions" about the issue of mountain bikes on the Front Country trails. For hikers and horse lovers, the main issues seemed to be safety and trail erosion; for mountain bikers it was equal access. Surprisingly, the discussions were relatively amicable.

By the second meeting, on October 3, five problem areas had been delineated. Providing better education about proper trail use and bridging the communication gap existing between bikers and hikers was a big concern. How to keep what everyone agreed was a small group of bikers from speeding down the trails was a second issue. A third concern, especially important to the Forest Service, was ensuring that Forest trails would meet everyone's recreational needs. The fourth, and main, problem area for hikers and equestrian groups, was trying to figure out how to keep the trails safe for everyone and at the same time making sure that excessive erosion didn't occur. The fifth problem area, a main worry of mountain bikers, was whether hiker or equestrian groups would support any compromise.

The third and fourth meetings (October 24 and November 14), like the earlier ones, were spent in intense but even-tempered discussions, developing alternatives that might help resolve issues posed by the problem areas listed above. The brainstorming led to development of a list of twenty-two different possibilities, ranging from limiting mountain bikes to designated trails to limiting them to certain times or days.

By the fifth meeting, held on December 5, the list had been pared to nine alternatives. Everyone present was asked to come back to the next meeting with their own personal recommendation. Santa Barbara District Ranger Pat Pontes asked that everyone be as reasonable as possible. When deciding which alternative they would be willing to support, he told the assembled group to ask themselves: "Will it be fair? Does it address aesthetic, erosion, and safety concerns? Can it be managed? Can we afford it? Does it take into account future growth of trail use? Is it legal? Above all he asked, does it represent a solution that everyone can live with?"

As the sixth meeting, held on January 23, 1986, got underway everyone sat quietly in their seats, members of each group wondering what those in the other groups were thinking. After months of discussion they were finally getting down to the nitty-gritty.

At the outset of the meeting Pontes asked that the focus be limited just to the Front Country trails. He explained that it was the Forest Service's feeling that this was the most controversial area, and as such should be dealt with first. Then he opened up a flip chart. On it were the five alternatives:

*Keep the status quo but provide an intensive program to educate trail users
*Close all trails to mountains bikes
*Regulate mountain bike use on certain trails
*Allow uphill bike travel on all trails and designate certain trails for downhill use
*Construct new trails for mountain bike use and disallow them on existing trails

Pontes then asked those present to break into small groups and to discuss which alternative or alternatives they felt should be applied to each of the Front Country trails. In making choices he asked each group to use four specific criteria: Does it provide for user safety? It is manageable and understandable? Will it meet user needs? Does it provide for resource protection?

A Rift Develops

After only a few minutes it became apparent that a serious rift was developing among those present. Tempers were becoming somewhat strained. Voices were being raised. During the previous meetings, though a lot of ground had been covered and a lot of good ideas had been generated, most of it had been of a general nature—that is, talking about problems and issues, rather than discussing how they would be applied to specific trails.

Now that representatives of the various groups were being asked to decide on a trail-by-trail basis what should be done, emotions began to surface. It seemed that every hiker had a "favorite trail" that they didn't want mountain bikers on. A major roadblock to reaching a reasonable compromise had finally surfaced—the inability of some hikers or horse riders to agree to any compromise.

At this point Forest Service officials realized that their hopes of negotiating a settlement everyone could agree to was probably not going to happen. After more heated discussion, during which some people felt that there wasn't any reason to continue on, Supervisor deHoll persuaded the group to try once more, this time focusing just on Alternative 3—the regulation of mountain bikes on some trails. Everyone was asked to come back again for a seventh meeting on March 6 to present their conclusions.

On that date each group—equestrian, hiker, and bicycle—was asked to present a report stating their position. The Equestrian presentation made it clear that they didn't favor use of any of the trails by mountain bikers. "There are almost no safe trails left for us to use," they said. "The trails are too narrow; the danger is too great. Trail by trail we're being forced out of the Front Country. We would only consider bike use on the trail sections below the Edison power lines, but not above them."

Hikers were somewhat divided, though the majority agreed with the horse group—all Front Country trails should be closed to mountain bike use. The overriding concern expressed in their report was safety. "The speed differential between hikers and bikers is just too great," the hikers explained.

Mountain bikers, of course, wanted the trails to remain open. "Education and enforcement of existing laws is the answer, not restrictions," they argued. "Develop a Code of Ethics, create a map that provides safety information and distribute it at the ranger stations, bike shops and even at trailheads. Collect more data, they urged. We still haven't proven that there really is a problem."

"The meeting was concluded," one ranger said, "with a very weary group who felt that agreement among participants was impossible and that it was time for the Forest Service to make its own decision." After seven long months of effort this, it seemed, was the only thing everyone could agree on.

A Final Symposium

On April 3 the Symposium was held an eighth and final time. Positions had not shifted. Everyone was still of the opinion that it was the Forest Service's job to make a decision. For the present, the Forest Service said that it would maintain the status quo, while in the meantime developing an educational program and collecting more data.

Two committees were established to help the Forest Service with this task—an Education Committee and a Data Committee. It was agreed that their work would be completed by May, forwarded to the Forest Service, and then sent out to all those who had participated in the Symposium for their comments. Then everyone would meet again in the Fall.

The Fall Meeting

As the different people began to assemble in the upstairs conference room at the Forest Service headquarters, they wondered what the Forest Service decision would be. It had been six months since the last meeting, and no one was quite sure what would happen. Everyone found out soon enough.

A mockup of a mountain biking map for the Front Country was presented by Forest Service representatives. Almost immediately it became clear that there would be no trail closures at this time. Educating mountain bikers about the problem through the use of this map, trail monitoring, and contact with the bike shops in town would be the policy.

Some hikers' mouths stood open. A few gasped. Others were angry. Some felt betrayed. There were threats of a lawsuit if anyone were to be hurt on one of the trails. A prominent member of one of the hiking groups stood up, trembling visibly. "These trails are not safe, and you know it," he told the Forest officials. "If anyone is hurt—or god forbid—is killed by a mountain bike, the blood will be on your hands."

Front Country Mountain Bike Survey

In the midst of this tension I asked, "How do you plan on getting the information you need?" While everyone seemed to think that getting more data was a good idea, and some had already been collected by the Data Committee, no one really had the time or manpower to go about it systematically. "Why not use my University class?" I suggested.

For six weeks, the eighty-odd students in the UCSB class, entitled "Management Issues: the Los Padres National Forest" spent afternoons and weekends stationed at the main trailheads leading into the Santa Ynez Mountains—the Jesusita, Tunnel, Rattlesnake, Cold Springs, Hot Springs, San Ysidro, and Romero trails. More than 1100 responses were gathered and then tabulated by the Forest Service.

The results were surprising. While most trail users had seen or encountered a mountain bike on one of the trails, 90% of the respondents believed the bikers to be polite and did not feel they should be banned from the trails.

Mountain bikers, of course, applauded the survey, while hikers, and especially the Sierra Club, took an extremely dim view of the results. "We're very disappointed," Anne Van Tyne, a spokeswoman for the Club, said after the results were made public. "We don't feel the study showed sufficient concern for safety." Some disappointed hikers sarcastically called it the "UC-BS Survey". A letter to the editor of the Santa Barbara

News-Press was to the point. "Hikers-and-Bikers Survey Took a False Trail," was the title of a letter from Paul Jacobs.

"I believe that surveys should be taken by people who are impartial," he argued, "this one was not! Let's face it: the UCSB students are more sympathetic towards cyclists (who are closer to their own age) than they are to hikers, who are more representative of older people, who symbolize repression.

"I think that the Sierra Club should take a survey, and submit the results to Ranger Pontes. I am sure that the results would contradict the UCSB survey."

The partiality or impartiality of these students can be argued back-and-forth, but the results were relatively clear (89% of those surveyed were hikers)—though almost all of the hikers reported at least one encounter with a bicycle on a Forest trail, very few of the bicyclists had caused them a problem. Eighty-nine percent of those surveyed felt the mountain bikers they encountered to be friendly, courteous, and safe. In fact, far more reported that their experience had been diminished by seeing trash on the trails than by the bicyclists.

Of the more than 1100 responses, only 42 surveys noted encounters with discourteous bikers. And just 65 surveys recounted unsafe incidents. No one reported seeing or experiencing an accident or injury resulting from an encounter either between a mountain biker and a hiker or a mountain biker and a horse rider during the six-week period. Ironically, the only accident reported was between mountain bikers.

If not as accurate as a professional survey might have been, the trend was clear. The average hiker did not believe either that the trails were unsafe or that mountain bikers were destroying their experience.

Kepner-Trego Analysis

On August, 1987 the Forest Service released a detailed analysis prepared by the Santa Barbara Ranger District entitled the "Kepner-Trego Analysis: Mountain Bicycle Situation on Santa Barbara Front Country Trails Man-

aged by the U.S. Forest Service". This was the first report of
its kind anywhere in the U.S. and relied heavily on the data
provided by my University class.

"The real problem to focus on," the study said, "is 'Do Safety
Hazards on the Santa Barbara Front Warrant Mt. Bicycle
Regulation?'" No, the Forest Service concluded. "It appears
the best choice is to continue with Current Management and
improve on trail safety, signing and user education as opportunities arise."

Dissatisfied by the the Forest Service response, a few days
after the K-T Analysis was issued, mountain bike opponents
approached the City Parks Department and asked that
Rattlesnake Trail be closed to mountain bikers. Because some
portions of the trail passed over land owned by the city of Santa
Barbara, a ban on their use in these sections would effectively
ban them on the entire length of the trail. Eventually the
Parks Department voted 5-1 for such closure, and on October
21, 1987 the City Council voted 7-0 to close the trail to bicycles.

To date, it is the only trail closed to bicycles in the County,
with the exception of those inside the wilderness areas.

Mountain Bike Survey is Updated

To see if there had been any shift in attitude among front
country trail users in regards to mountain bikes (and if the
original survey had been accurate) I decided to ask my class to
conduct a similar survey two years later.

They were taken from April 20 to June 6, 1989. Approximately 60 students participated and all front country trails
(Jesusita, Tunnel, Rattlesnake, Cold Springs, Hot Springs,
San Ysidro, and Romero) were included. Due to its high
equestrian use and concerns about appropriateness of mountain bikes on it, the Santa Cruz Trail in the Upper Oso area
was also included in the survey.

A total of 573 surveys were completed during the period.
Several of these represented the combined response of more
than one person. As a result there was a total of slightly more
than 600 responses.

Because it was done not so much to gain baseline data but to determine what shift might have occurred in the intervening period, questions were focused directly on attitudes that trail users had about mountain bike use on the trails.

A widespread belief held among most people surveyed in 1987 had been that bicycle use was okay at that time, but could be a problem in the future if use increased.

Indeed, the 1989 survey did show a marked increase in the number of mountain bike users on the trails. The increase was dramatic—use of the front country trails by mountain bikers increased from 7% to 24.4%. Hiker contact with mountain bikers had also increased quite a bit, with almost 50% of trail users having four or more experiences with bicyclists on the trails. Did it mean there was now a serious safety problem with mountain bikes on the Front Country trails? Did this mean that bikes were no longer welcome there?

Given the increase in bicycle use and hiker contact with them, it would be expected that safety concerns would have increased dramatically. In fact, this was not the case. The Survey results were almost identical to those from 1987.

But while concerns about safety didn't increase, the survey did show that more and more trail users were becoming concerned about possible trail damage and erosion caused by the bikes. Many hikers provided detailed information on the back of their surveys about trail rutting, destruction of switchbacks, and obliteration of water bars that they had seen.

What had been a safety issue two years ago was now turning into a focus on resource protection. "Protecting the trails is a major problem," says District Ranger Pat Pontes. "We've got enough money right now to maintain the trails, but not if the erosion gets accelerated."

Interestingly, trail damage may actually become the issue in future years which eliminates mountain bikes from the Front Country. As money for trail maintenance dries up, there may come a point where the Forest Service, will simply no longer be able to afford having them on the trail.

Future of the Front Country Trails

Personally, I've always maintained that we should leave the Front Country trails to the hikers. Like mountain bikers, hikers also treasure the ability to escape from the city's confines for a few hours. The Front Country provides them with a system of trails that makes it possible to do so.

One of the incredibly special things about Santa Barbara is the proximity of the trails to the city boundaries. There are but six escape routes leading from the mechanized world into the Santa Ynez Mountains. That means escape from bikes as well as city noise, traffic jams, pollution, and time clocks. These are precious and needed. They should remain inviolate.

But I've never thought that the only alternative was a blanket policy etched in stone banning them from the entire front side of the range. We don't need more rules. We need more people who are caring and sensitive, who care for the land, and whose actions are reflective of that caring.

Recently, though, I've started to wonder. Is it time we call an end to mountain bike use on the front side? Should the Forest Service take a more restrictive position? Not too long ago I received a letter from a friend. He's a dentist, a person I respect a lot, and has been a member of the County Riding and Hiking Trails Advisory Committee for quite awhile. His name is Art.

"Last Sunday I went riding [by horse] in San Roque Canyon on the Jesusita Trail," Art wrote. "I had not ridden the Jesusita Trail in about 6 months, and I was shocked to see the terrible devastation, due to the heavy usage by mountain bikers—it is destroying this once beautiful trail.

"The switchbacks have been especially damaged. There is not one water bar left. They have been pounded out of existence. In a number of places the trail resembles a ditch. Tread in a number of places has been knocked down so badly that one of our horses lost its footing and collapsed with our young guest. Luckily, neither was injured.

"As we were going up the trail, a biker came down at an excessive speed, but luckily saw us in time to slow down, otherwise, it could have been a disaster. When the Forest Service held its hearings, I was one of those trail users that consented to giving the mountain bike people a chance to use the trails, to see how things would work out.

"Now, after seeing how damaging mountain bikers are to trails, plus the danger they pose when speeding, I am convinced that they are incompatible with trails.

"Unless there is a real change in how some—even if they are only a few—use the trails, perhaps it is time to ban them from the Front Country."

A Letter from the District Ranger

Not too long after receiving this letter, the Santa Barbara District Ranger, Pat Pontes, authored a letter of warning to the mountain bike community, an expression of his dissatisfaction with Front Country use by bikers. The letter dated April 16, 1989, was distributed to bike shops in an effort to get the message out.

"I am writing a personal note to alert you to a developing problem that exists on the Santa Barbara Front forest trail system," he said. "Some bicyclists are riding downhill at an excessive speed! Your continued use of these trails is in jeopardy.

"During the last few months we have found some groups of bicyclists are riding down hill on the trails and up on the bank's edge/slope above the trail tread. This is causing an eyebrow effect, and soil is eroding onto the trail. Also the braking action of fast riders is causing mechanical erosion in the tread (a U-shaped depression) that is difficult to water bar. Some individuals are beginning to cut switchbacks, locking their brakes downward to the trail below. This severely damages the trail by causing accelerated soil erosion and water channeling....

"I am concerned that we are close to meeting the criteria for bicycle regulation on some trails."

As trail use increases, so do the number of potential conflicts. Every mountain biker needs to ride in a way that not only shows respect for the land but other trail users as well. Minimum impact is essential.

 # A Code of Ethics

"Responsibility deals with our respect for the total environment, including people. Responsibility is a basic attitude, our environmental style to put it in a slightly different perspective."

Hank Barlow
Mountain Bike Magazine

Despite what some people seem to think, the Los Padres National Forest is not your personal playground, to do with as you please. It is a sensitive part of nature's system and it needs your care.

A mountain bike makes it possible to explore a much wider area of the Forest than is often possible on foot. There are incredible places to see and to experience here—hidden sandstone narrows, deep pools, hot springs, high country filled with pine forests, wild places that defy description.

A mountain bike is a means to these places and experiences. If used carelessly, they can damage and destroy—both the natural resource and other people's experiences.

There is no long standing tradition of mountain bike use on trails or jeep roads in the backcountry. They are not part of our pioneer heritage as are foot and horse travel. To be accepted as a legitimate part of the trail user community, they must be used with sensitivity and care.

Whenever possible, I would recommend that you use the trails and dirt roads found on the crest and other side of the Santa Ynez Mountains, rather than the Front Country to avoid conflict with other users.

With this in mind I would appreciate your thinking about the following points while you are out in the backcountry enjoying your mountain bike.

Ride to enjoy the beauty and excitement and share your enthusiasm with others.

Ride in a way that cares for the land and its inhabitants. It is their home.

Practice riding techniques that provide a minimum of impact.

Ride with other trail users in mind and enhance rather than interfere with their enjoyment.

Use a bell, a whistle, or a friendly hello to signal your presence.

Always assume that someone is around the corner.

When approaching equestrians, dismount and ask them what they want you to do.

Understand that you are a spokesperson for all bike riders, whether you want to be or not.

Smile and say something friendly to everyone you encounter.

Know when to walk your bike. The trails will appreciate your caution.

Recognize your own limits and ride within them. You will be safer and the resource will be better protected for it.

Good braking means never having to skid. If you don't know how to ride on trails in an environmentally sensitive way, ask for help in learning how.

Cyclist's Code of Responsibility

To help develop a more responsible attitude, the Forest Service has created a code of ethics which it would like you to obey when you are in the Los Padres National Forest.

Regardless of where you ride please follow them to help ensure that as many trails as possible remain open to mountain bike use.

Bicycles are not allowed in wilderness areas.

Yield the right-of-way to other trail users. Horses may spook when they see an unfamiliar object, especially one that moves quickly and quietly. Realize that people judge all cyclists by your actions.

Slow down and use caution when passing others. If necessary, dismount your bike on the downhill side of the trail and wait for horses or hikers to pass.

Control your speed at all times. Approach turns in anticipation of someone being around the bend. Cross water bars at a slow speed rather than running up on the bank and around them.

Walk your bike around switchbacks rather than locking up your rear brake and sliding around them. Locked brakes lead to trail erosion and rutting. Avoid cutting across the inner edge of a switchback.

Stay on designated roads and trails to avoid damaging the native vegetation. Wheel ruts channel water and can cause erosion.

Allow trails to dry out before you use them.

Don't disturb wildlife or livestock.

Pack out what you pack in. Wherever possible, help clean up trash that has been carelessly left behind.

Observe signs prohibiting bicycle use. Some trails cross private property and are subject to deed restrictions which prohibit vehicle travel of any kind.

Extend common courtesy to all trail users.

THANKS!

 # Wilderness & Mountain Bikes

For many of us who get out into the backcountry as often as we can, a mountain bike is the vehicle that allows us the opportunity to re-acquaint ourselves with nature and to re-establish a relationship that seems to get blasted to hell and back in the city. In our increasingly urbanized and technological society it is a relationship that is tenuous at best.

Because of its link to technology and the potential for abuse, mountain biking is under attack from some environmental groups—notably the Sierra Club—which is dedicated to the proposition that no trail should be violated by the fat track of a mountain bike.

Some would say that you don't see anything on a mountain bike. You are going too fast. Not true.

There is an indefinable dimension to mountain biking. "In mountain biking, the background chattering of the mind is silenced," Hank Barlow writes. "Life becomes the passage, not the destination."

Sometimes I think we are too caught up in detail. We see things while ignoring the form, the essence of which things are made. To experience nature fully is to integrate—sounds, smells, textures, soft shadings, intricate patterns, and delicate emotions. It is to learn patience, practice humility, express joy, and to share it with others.

The vehicle is the means, not the end; to experience, not just see, the goal—a "celebration of living" is what Barlow calls it—a zest for life and a relationship with it that transcends the vehicle used.

Backpackers enjoying the solitude offered in upper Sulphur Springs Canyon which is located in the San Rafael Wilderness. Wilderness areas are closed to mountain bikes. Please respect this.

It is that the state of mind one brings to the experience, not the vehicle, that determines the quality of the experience. On foot, on horseback, or on bike, we can all share in the mystical and magical world of nature—and we can support each other in doing so.

Perhaps the greatest challenge for all environmental groups is to find common grounds and common means of supporting each other, and to find positive ways to work together so that we can all be winners, including our natural environment.

Do Mountain Bikes Belong in Wilderness?

Perhaps I'm in the minority of mountain bikers, but I strongly believe that wilderness needs more people who cherish its wildness and fewer who would mechanize it. Despite what mountain bikes offer, there comes a point when you've got to get off your bike and experience the world directly, as up close as possible. No ifs, ands or buts about it.

We've come too far, too fast. In a world light years from that of the Chumash, one altered inexorably by modern man, we need simply to say no to technology in the wilderness. Too many compromises have already been made.

Fundamental to wilderness is the relationship between time and space, a relationship that is increasingly distorted by man's preoccupation with speed. On a basic level, the faster we travel through an area the less real space we have available to us; on a more subtle level we also alter how we relate to wilderness.

If all we were talking about was recreation, I wouldn't have any problem with mountain bikes in wilderness. But we aren't. Wilderness is not just another recreational opportunity.

Wilderness is about re-creating the fundamental conditions given to us as a human species. It is a place to walk softly while we try to figure out how we got here and where we're heading. It is that place out there where you've got to get off your bike.

It's part of the same reason why we cherish the Chumash rock art and do what we can to protect it. It is a direct connection to a world of primeval conditions that we as a species will never be able to know or re-create again. Once lost, like our youth, there are some things that can never be regained.

Can We Have Both?

In Santa Barbara we are fortunate to have a topography that allows us the luxury of both having the San Rafael and Dick Smith Wildernesses—and enough country outside of those two areas for mountain bikers to enjoy their own relationship with nature.

Please leave the wilderness areas to those who would like to experience them by foot travel.

Being Prepared

"The core of any adventure—and that's what mountain biking is ultimately about—is looking with an unjaundiced eye at the risks involved and weighing those risks against the potential rewards, tangible or experiential. The key to overcoming those risks is being prepared to independently deal with them. Adventure—at least for most Americans—is leaving his or her society's immediate support systems behind and interacting with the world one on one. Backcountry adventure is synonymous with self-reliance."

Hank Barlow
Mountain Bike Magazine

A favorite afternoon trip of mine is an out and back to Gibraltar Mine. From Lower Oso the ride is moderate, 5 miles on pavement, 3 miles along the Santa Ynez River to the dam, and then and additional 4.5 miles to the rusting ruins of the quicksilver mine. It's a good workout and I've probably done it thirty times or more in the past few years. I've never had a problem along the way, either. Until a recent trip.

I always thought it would be great to ride the length of Gibraltar Lake and as the level of the reservoir began to get lower and lower I finally had the chance. It was Christmas vacation, 1990, and all that remained of the lake was a small puddle directly behind the dam. I followed the usual route to the mine, the dirt road that skirts the south side of the reservoir.

I explored around the smelting equipment a bit as I usually do and then started coasting down to the lake. The surface was crusty and hard, with plenty of support for the fat tires on my bike. I can do this, I thought. The only serious problem seemed to be keeping my front tire from dropping down into the deep cracks created when the mud on the lake bottom had dried out. Some of them measured more than 6 inches in width and 2 feet in depth. I could visualize myself dropping into one of them and going headfirst over the handlebars.

Perhaps I was concentrating too much on the cracks and not enough on the low brush that was starting to grow out on the river flats. Without any warning a branch caught in my chain near the derailleur and before I could stop pedaling (I was standing up and in the midst of a hard downstroke) I heard a snap. Suddenly there was slack in the chain and I was freewheeling. I looked down at my rear wheel in horror. The derailleur was dangling near the ground, with part of the branch still stuck in it.

Now, I used to carry a spare derailleur around with me. Along with a few other (heavy) tools and spare parts that I'd never needed to use. I left the spare axle behind first, as well as the cone wrenches that fit it. Then I threw out the extra brake lever, figuring I could always make it home with one brake. One day, finally, I stopped carrying the extra derailleur.

Right then I was thinking, "Geeze, Ray, I wish you hadn't done that." But I had. What to do?

It was 3pm (it gets dark at 5), I was alone, and it was at least 11 miles back to the car. I jerry-rigged the chain, but it would barely work. Every time I put much pressure on my pedals it would slip off the rear cogs. I saved a little distance by going straight down to the dam, but the mud cracks were a pain. Where I could, I stood on one pedal and pushed (as a skate-boarder would) with the other foot. I walked the uphills and coasted the downhills, getting to Red Rock at 4pm. My bad luck held—there was no one left there to hitch a ride from. Finally I made it to Lower Oso at 5:15pm, plenty tired and perhaps a little bit wiser.

Preparing Adequately

In the Santa Barbara backcountry, preparing adequately means being equipped to deal with almost anything that may come along—whether this means handling a first aid problem, route finding on your topographical map, or fixing a broken part on your bike. Ultimately, it means making reasonable assumptions about what to expect on your trip and preparing accordingly.

Often, acting responsibly is determined as much by what you choose not to do as it is by what you choose to do.

THE DO'S

Bring along enough water and food to satisfy your body's needs. That means 2 quarts of water at an absolute minimum and more in the summer. Know where safe sources of water can be found in the backcountry and bring along a pocket filter to protect yourself from giardia.

Carry first aid equipment and know how to use it. At a minimum bring bandages, gauze, sterile pads, tape and one or more ace bandages, antibiotic cream, betadyne solution, Que-tips, and eye drops are a good idea.

Don't rely on an already opened tube of glue if you need to patch a tire. Too often they dry out and are unusable. Carry an unopened tube and use it only if the opened one has hardened.

Bring along a spare piece of sidewall from an old bike tire. If you have a blowout, you can reinforce the tire on your bike by putting this inside between the tube and the place where you've had the blowout. In an emergency, duct tape and a piece of cardboard will work.

Carry a brand new spare tube with you. Patch any flat tire first and only use the new spare if you have to.

Know enough about your bike so that you can make minor adjustments to it. Tools won't help if you can't use them.

THE DON'TS

Don't get in over your head. Keep your trips within the level of your ability and the shape you are in. Start on short rides if you are inexperienced or you need to get in better shape. Santa Barbara has a lot of mountainous country and you need to be prepared for the long uphills on some of the rides. Get in shape on road rides described in this book and you'll be ready for the long backcountry rides.

Stay off most of the trails after it has rained. While many of them can be ridden, a lot of the trails also pass through sections of heavy clay. Not only will your bike clog up with so much mud that you will end up carrying it, but you'll have a lovely time trying to clean it afterwards. Be kind to the trails and leave them alone for 4-5 days after rain.

Don't forget rain gear if there is any chance of precipitation. Hypothermia is a serious concern in the backcountry. On a bike you are completely exposed to the elements and wind chill is a factor, especially when you are coasting down long hills.

Don't ride alone, especially on the longer loops, unless you are sure you can deal with any emergency that might come up.

The Basics

It is tough to know exactly what to bring along. The whole purpose of a backcountry adventure can be ruined if you are burdened down with enough equipment to prepared you for every situation. Freedom is having the weight of civilization lifted from your shoulders. What do bring then?

There are some things you just shouldn't leave home without. You can put together a basic tool kit which covers just about all of the basic situations you'll find yourself in that will fit in a small pouch beneath your bike seat. Why be foolish?

Spare Tube	Socket—8, 9, 10mm
Patch Kit	Spoke Wrench
Set of Tire Levers	Chain Breaker
Crescent Wrench	Spare Brake Cable
Small Screw Driver	Spare Derailleur Cable
Allen Wrenches—3, 4, 5, 6mm	Spare Nuts & Bolts

Others things that you should include, either in your day pack or fanny pack or on your bike.

Pump (an absolute must)
Minimum of 2 Quarts of Water
First Aid Kit
Swiss Army Knife
Flashlight
Spare Batteries
Map(s)
Whistle
Duct tape
Small piece of sidewall
Chain Lube
Sun Protection
Lip Balm
Rain Gear
Extra Clothes

For overnight trips or long day trips, of course you can prepare for the worst by bringing practically everything you own. The following list are those extra things you might think of including if you have room or dread being stuck out in nowhere without the proper tool or equipment.

Spare Derailleur (of course)
Extra Spokes
A Set of Crank Bearings
Spare Axle
Cone/Pedal Wrenches
Crank Puller
Spare Chain (or links)

Oh, by the way. There are no buses in the backcountry and the local 7-11 is a long, long ways away. Prayers or curses don't help much either. Be prepared to make do all by yourself.

While there are a few things to avoid in the Santa Barbara front and backcountry, the one that seems to cause the most problems is poison oak. Be sure you know what it looks like and ride slowly in areas you suspect it might be lurking, such as in shaded canyons.

What to Avoid

Despite a few unpleasant aspects out on the trail, especially those pesky flies, there are only four things you really need to look out for in the Santa Barbara front and backcountry while you are out on a mountain bike ride—Rattlesnakes, Ticks, Poison Oak, and the Water.

Poison Oak

There are probably more myths concerning poison oak than just about any other backcountry problem. No you don't get it from scratching. The mugwort probably won't work. No, it can't get in your bloodstream and spread. Yes, you can get it from the branches, even if all the leaves have fallen off, as in the wintertime.

Simply put, you get poison oak by coming into contact with the offending bush, whether in leaf or stick form. What causes the irritation is the oil, a sappy, whitish liquid known as the Rhus antigen, which was named after its discoverer. All the plants which cause this reaction (such as poison oak, poison ivy, or sumac) have the same basic oil. The reaction to all of them is known by the same name—Rhus dermatitis.

Only those areas which come into contact with the oil will react and only to the extent that they are sensitive to it (why some people have sensitive skin and others don't I will never understand. I'm just glad I'm not). While the ability to react is somewhat determined by genetics (if your mom and dad get it you probably will too), repeated contact with the oil can increase your sensitivity. Don't brag about how you can crash right through the stuff. You may regret it later.

Contact can be direct, from the plant leaves and vines, or indirect, by coming into contact with the oil at a later time, either from contaminated clothes or perhaps from man's best friend—your dog. An absolutely awful way to get it is through inhalation of the vapors, such as from a trash fire or while sitting around a warm, toasty campfire stoked by someone's careless use of of poison oak for kindling. Ever thought of what oak might be like on the inside of your mouth or throat? Or to wake up in the morning with your eyes swollen shut? Once the rash breaks out (usually in about 3 days) scratching will make the blisters run but the fluid released by your incessant itching is serum, not the Rhus oil. You might infect the area but you won't cause the oak to spread.

Surprisingly, neither antihistamine creams nor calamine lotions stop the reaction. All they do is help keep the itching down and help stop the fluid from running once you've started scratching. If a few blisters do appear after a trip into the mountains, they can be treated with any brand of over-the-counter cortisone cream and a good antihistamine, such as Benadryl (dephenhydramine). The rash should be gone in a week. If not, consult your doctor.

What should you do if you think you've made contact with this obnoxious plant (there must be some reason of its existence, but though I've tried, I haven't come up with one yet). There are a number of things you can do. First of all, get the clothes you were wearing off as soon as is practical and keep them separated. Then take a long shower, starting off with as cool water as you can handle (this helps keep your pores closed), and wash yourself as thoroughly as possible. Wash your clothes by themselves with a potent detergent—cycle them through twice if you want to be sure to get the oil off.

Best advice? My rule of thumb is, "If you can't tell what it is—whether leaf, stick, vine, or bush—don't touch it."

Ticks and Lyme Disease

It used to be that all you had to worry about when it came to ticks was a gross-out or two, especially if you missed one on the periodic "body checks" that are necessary in the backcountry, and you were forced to use a pair of tweezers (a handy item, even on day hikes) to twist one out.

But today, Lyme disease has everyone worried. This tick-borne bacterial infection is spreading faster than any other ailment with the exception of AIDS. It has been reported in 46 states and afflicted more than 30,000 in the US last year.

Lyme disease is caused by a spiral bacterium spread to animals and humans by ticks. When the tiny creatures bite they can inject the organism into you. One of the characteristics of ticks which make them a perfect host for such a disease is their ability to transmit microorganisms from one generation of ticks to the next. At the site of the bite, a red, circular rash with a clearing in the center appears. A few days or weeks after the bite, flu-like symptoms may appear, as well as pain in the joints. If untreated the symptoms can spread to the nervous system and cause aching in the joints similar to arthritis.

Lyme disease can be cured if treated early through the use of penicillin or other antibiotics. Unfortunately, because the tick bite may not be noticed or possibly because the symptoms are vague enough either to be ignored or mis-diagnosed, the disease is often not treated quickly enough. While rarely fatal or long lasting, it can cause chronic symptoms that are difficult to get rid of.

Fortunately for us, the main areas where this disease has been contracted are east of the Rockies, in the Midwest and Northeast, especially New York. Still, you can minimize the danger of your contracting Lyme disease (or being bitten by any tick). A vaccine for dogs is available though there is some concern among physicians about its long term effect or safety. For more information consult your physician.

You'll find ticks in some areas and some time frames more than others. Narrow trails, especially those with grass fringes that you can rub against, such as the Matias Potrero Trail, are prime tick areas. The period between March and June is tick season, though you'll find them (or more accurately, they'll find you) throughout the year. One way to help is to dress and act accordingly.

Pants tucked into your socks will help keep them off your legs and light-colored clothing will help you spot them. An insect repellant such as DEET can help repel them. Above all, a full body check should be done every half hour or so, more often in areas of heavy infestation.

Despite these precautions, should you find one beginning to burrow in, don't panic. A tick takes a number of hours to latch on and ready itself to feed. It may be as much as 24 hours before it is capable of transmitting a bacterial infection to you.

To remove the tick place the tips of your tweezers over the mouth parts, as close to the skin as you can get them. This lessens the danger of pulling off the body and leaving the mouth parts behind. Pull steadily away from the skin extremely slowly until the tick lets go. I've always had good success twisting counterclockwise while pulling (I've been told they bore into you in a clockwise direction). If the head stays in it should work itself out in a few days. If not, see your doctor.

Afterwards wash the bite area, apply a disinfectant, and cover with a bandaid.

Rattlesnakes

There are 31 species of rattlesnakes in the Western Hemisphere (a comforting thought), 6 of them found in California. Fortunately, only one of them resides in Santa Barbara County—the Western Pacific Rattlesnake—known under its Latin name as *Crotalus viridis*, a name that is more benign than its bite.

Rattlesnakes are known as pit vipers because they have small holes, or pits, on either side of their triangular-shaped heads, just under their eyes, in which infra red receptors are lodged, enabling them to track their warm-blooded prey. A thin heat-sensitive membrane covers the back of these pit organs. The angle at which heat passes through the small holes and strikes the membrane provides a sort of solar radar tracking system. Rattlesnakes actually don't see very well.

The Western Pacific Rattlesnake inhabits a variety of habitats ranging in elevation from sea level to 6,000', which means you can find them anywhere in the County (another comforting thought). Personally I've sat near the top of San Rafael Peak and watched one of them warm up in the morning sun, so I know they're everywhere. The peak is 6200' in elevation.

Because they are cold-blooded, rattlesnakes are dependent on the environment for heat rather than relying on their metabolism to provide it. In the Santa Barbara area, where winters aren't severe, they hibernate singly or in small numbers from late November through early March (this is good news, folks!). This means that you only have to worry about them from mid-March through the start of October.

Soon after awakening in the spring, rattlesnakes mate, giving birth a litter of from 6-to-12 live little ones, which are active almost immediately. Because they are inexperienced, they are the ones most often seen in the daytime.

Where will you find the Western Pacific Rattlesnake? Usually on rocky outcrops, rocky ledges, brush-covered slopes, rocky streams, and wherever you find piles of brush or debris. I'm always wary when passing the cone-shaped nest built by the pack rat. I figure there's a rattlesnake lurking somewhere, waiting patiently for a tasty meal.

In the Santa Barbara area, rattlesnake coloring varies. Blotches that range from light brown to a dark black run the length of the snake, making it look like it has a diamond-covered topside. While the lighter colored ones are extremely beautiful, those that are almost black are menacing looking and seem to have an evil aura about them.

It has taken me a long time to accept the fact that these creatures play an important role in nature and deserve to be left alone.

Though the rattlesnake would prefer to rattle out a warning than strike, people do get bitten by them. Their range is about half the length of their body, usually a circular area about 1-2' in diameter, though every time I see one I'm sure it will be able to leap out and get me, even if I'm a safe 15 feet away. Each year about 20 people in the U.S. die from poisonous snake bites, mostly children and the elderly. Rattlesnakes account for about 60% of the bites and nearly all the fatalities. In the 30 years I've lived here, I only know of one person who died from a rattlesnake bite, but it can happen.

What should you do? While a number of remedies have been suggested over the years, ranging from use of snake bite and antivenom kits to cryotherapy (cold therapy), the most cautious—and probably best—treatment is to immobilize the affected part of the body using a splint and to keep the patient as calm and inactive as possible while heading to the nearest emergency room as quickly as possible.

So, what do you do when you've been bitten by a poisonous snake and you're hours from the nearest medical clinic? Don't get bitten in the first place! I can't say that enough. Watch where you walk. Watch where you put your hands and your feet. Look first before stepping over a log or putting your hand up on a rock or a ledge.

And if you should see a rattlesnake, appreciate it for what it is—a necessary part of nature's web of life—and stay clear. From afar, I've found that they are very beautiful creatures.

Water Purity in the Wilderness Areas

"Water has more life in it than
any part of the earth's surface."
Thoreau, Walden

Beware the crystal clear water—it may contain organisms known by the state of California to be harmful to your health. The culprit is known as *giardia* (pronounced gee-ar-de-a), a teeny-tiny protozoa that resides in the upper part of the small intestine, once ingested. Giardia has a life cycle that is composed of two stages. The first is the reproductive stage; the second the cyst, a stage in which the germ is encased in a hard shell.

It is the second stage which causes the problem. The cysts remain alive in even the coldest water for as long as 3 months, even when frozen (don't eat the yellow snow or even the stuff that looks as pure as Ivory flakes). As few as 10 of the little buggers can cause you to come down with giardiasis and if you've swallowed a hundred or more you'll get it for sure.

Giardia comes from animal droppings or in some cases from human waste (always bury your waste in a hole at least 8" deep and never, ever closer than 100 feet from any water source). As the animals wade or wallow in a stream or pool the droppings enter the water. In some cases rain may wash the animal wastes into it. When ingested, the water-borne cyst attaches itself to the wall of your upper small intestine and your stomach's heat activates it, causing it to go into the reproductive cycle, causing sickness and in the process producing more cysts.

Though not life threatening, the disorder (giardiasis) can be incapacitating, causing diarrhea, vomiting, gas (lots of it), loss of appetite, abdominal cramps, and bloating. These symptoms may last up to 6 weeks. In short, it's no fun.

Even if the water is clear, cold, and free running it may harbor giardia cysts. They have been found bubbling up from what appear to be the purest of springs. You can't tell if they are present by the taste. Nor by the smell, or the look of it. The usual amount of time between ingestion and the onset of symptoms is about 2 weeks, meaning that you won't know you've got it until quite awhile later and you might even mistake it for something else.

The best way to prevent the disorder is to bring enough water along with you so that you needn't depend on what nature offers. But this can be difficult to do on a long day hike and especially on a full day's mountain bike ride. Other than bringing your own along there are really only 3 other choices: boiling, filtering, or chemically treating it. The surest way to destroy the giardia cysts, as well as other organisms, is to boil the water for at least a minute, preferably 3-5 minutes to be safe. Chemical treatment by use of iodine or chlorine isn't considered as reliable as the use of heat, but it does provide a handy and relatively simple way to deal with the problem. Recent studies indicate that these chemicals may not work because they can't penetrate the cyst's hard shell. Use iodine rather than chlorine if you have a choice. It is more effective. Another drawback to use of these chemicals is that they make the water taste funny.

What may be the most practical choice (especially if you backpack) is the use of a filtration system to remove the cysts. "First Need", "H$_2$OK", and "Katadyn Pocket Filters" all have been tested by the EPA and found to work on the giardia cyst.

If an Emergency Occurs

The Los Padres Search and Rescue Team is a non-profit, all- volunteer organization that mobilizes when an emergency occurs in an area that normal rescue personnel cannot get into.

Should you get into trouble don't hesitate to seek out their help. You cannot contact the Team directly; it operates under the auspices of the Santa Barbara County Sheriff's office. Call 911 and tell them the nature of your situation. If warranted, they will transfer you to the command officer (known as the Watch Officer) at the Sheriff's office.

In case of an emergency inside the Los Padres National Forest, there is also a 24-hour emergency number which you can use. It is 967-3467.

If help is not immediately available, rather than trying to do something immediately, try to take a few moments to assess the situation and to develop a plan of action. Evaluate each of the possible alternatives you have available to you. If time permits, take time to talk out the pros and cons for each. Talk over the choices with each member of your group and try to reach a consensus that everyone feels comfortable with. Continue to evaluate the situation as conditions change.

 # The Mountain Crest

If I could create the perfect setting in which to live, it would be in the mountains, but they would be located not too far from the sea. The mountains would be tall and majestic, stretching for miles in either direction and just below them, ocean waves would lap against a narrow coastal plain. Out over the distant water I would place a long thin range of islands, several of them, just far enough away from shore to seem remote, yet close enough to create romantic dreams.

To the interior I would place more ranges of mountains, equally as far away as the islands so that they, too, would seem as wild and remote. In between there would be wide valleys with rolling grass-covered hills and the scattered crowns of majestic trees. From my view from the mountain top these valleys would turn brilliant green and golden orange in color after the spring rains.

Across the crest of these mountains I would add a long, thin ribbon of road and trails leading off of it so that I would have plenty of places to explore. But thank my blessings. I don't have to spend my time creating such a paradise—it is already here. The place lies just behind Santa Barbara—the top of the Santa Ynez Mountains.

The crest road that runs the length of the mountaintop, along with the dirt roads and trails leading down into the Santa Ynez Valley, form a mountain biker's paradise.

West Camino Cielo

In actuality, the road is not a single continuous route but is composed of two distinct sections: East and West Camino Cielo. West Camino Cielo begins a half-mile below the crest of

San Marcos Pass. Leading across the rugged and extremely remote western portion of the Santa Ynez Mountains, it snakes its way across a series of bony spines and high prominences for 17 miles to Refugio Pass where it ends. For five miles the road is paved, and the going is easy, but just beyond the entrance to a private gun club, the road abruptly turns to dirt and begins a series of sharp downhill switchbacks that seem to lead backward in time to a frontier era.

While there aren't a lot of different mountain bike routes in this area (only the Tequepis trail leads off the crest), the ride along the crest is spectacular. Beyond Lizard's Mouth, where the road turns to dirt, rarely will you encounter automobile traffic. As you ride, you not only have views in either direction but a remote and very primitive feeling the entire distance to Refugio Pass, if you choose to go that far. With a shuttle car in place you need not return the same way you've come. Actually you have a choice of three alternatives: dropping off the crest and riding down the Tequepis Trail to Cachuma Lake; taking Refugio Pass Road south to the state park at Refugio Beach; or turning north and dropping down the back side of the Santa Ynez Mountains on Refugio Pass Road and following it to Highway 246 (near Santa Ynez High School).

East Camino Cielo

The thin, winding middle portion of Camino Cielo also seems remote in nature, though not nearly so much as West Camino Cielo. It is paved across the entire 10-mile length from San Marcos Pass to Gibraltar Road and you'll more-than-likely see a lot more people along the way. Nevertheless it still provides a sense of adventure and a feeling of exhilaration on the drive or bike ride across. In addition there are plenty of places to stop and explore, have a picnic, or enjoy either the coastal or inlands views.

Along the way you'll find three routes down into the Santa Ynez Valley: the Synder Trail; Arroyo Burro Road; and the Angostura Pass Road—each providing marvelous mountain bike riding and numerous loop or shuttle possibilities. Along the crest there are numerous other sights as well: out and back rides on the Fremont Trail, to Painted Cave, or to the ruins at Knapp's Castle, or to the top of La Cumbre Peak.

A great adventure that you will remember for a long time is provided by riding the entire 10-mile section of East Camino to Gibraltar Road, and then continuing on this back down into town, an additional 7 miles of intense downhill. While hard core riders will turn up their noses if you start this ride from the Cielo Store (you'll need a shuttle for this or a friend to drive you to the top of San Marcos Pass), I just can't recommend the ride up Highway 154. Besides, this way you can take more time at stops along the way and really enjoy your trip.

Romero Saddle

East of Gibraltar Road, Camino Cielo takes on a different character. The road is almost level for the next 6 miles, and the feeling is much more like that on the West Camino section—remote and rugged. To the interior you are not looking at the Santa Ynez Valley, but steep, mountainous terrain that contains the Dick Smith Wilderness. In the distance you can see Big Pine Mountain and Madulce Peak, both over 6,500 in elevation. If you look carefully you can even see the rounded crest of Mt. Pinos which is over 60 miles away.

Beyond Romero Saddle the crest road turns primitive, becoming a bumpy dirt road that leads down into the upper Santa Ynez watershed where there are several overnight car camps and some of the best mountain bike riding you will find anywhere in Southern California.

Along this part of the crest you will find 2 routes that lead down into the upper Santa Ynez River canyon—the Forbush Flats and Blue Canyon trails—as well as several that will take you back down into Santa Barbara—the Cold Springs and San Ysidro trails. At the end of the paved section, you will also find Romero Road, an old dirt path that winds back and forth down into the Montecito foothills.

For a relaxing ride that encompasses this part of Camino Cielo, try parking on the crest near the top of Gibraltar Road and riding out to Romero Saddle and back. The views are spectacular on this 12 mile ride, and though you will have some uphill on the way back, it is relatively easy.

Camino Cielo Road Log

For those of you who want to combine a bike ride with a drive, hike, or picnic on one of the sections of Camino Cielo you will find that all of them provide a worthwhile afternoon's outing. Beautiful views of the islands and the coastline on the south side of the road and the Santa Ynez Valley, the San Rafael Mountains, and wilderness areas on the north, make the crest of the Santa Ynez Mountains truly a bicyclist's paradise.

West Camino—San Marcos Pass to Refugio Pass

0.0 Cielo Store. Here you can purchase last minute supplies as well as relax with folks who live in the neighborhood. The store carries a wide variety of cool drinks, food, and local crafts.

0.1 San Marcos Pass

0.2 Kinevan Road. This leads down the upper end of San Jose Creek through a beautiful narrow canyon to West Camino Cielo.

1.0 West Camino Cielo. The turn is sharply to the right and up out of the canyon

3.6 Trail to the Playground (see trail description). You won't find the trail marked nor exact directions as to how to get there, but if you find the Playground you'll be glad you took the time.

4.8 Lizard's Mouth (see trail description). A beautiful field of boulders just a quarter of a mile off the road. You will find the trailhead just before the Winchester Gun Club.

5.0   Road turns to dirt and drops down 500' in elevation to a saddle which marks the beginning of the main dirt section of West Camino Cielo (see trail description).

12.0 Tequepis Trail turnoff, which is just before Broadcast Peak. The trail leads down to Lake Cachuma (see description).

17.0 Refugio Pass

East Camino—San Marcos Pass to Gibraltar Road
0.0 San Marcos Pass

0.2 Cielo Store. Here you can purchase last minute supplies as well as relax with folks who live in the neighborhood. The store carries a wide variety of cool drinks, food, and local crafts.

1.75 The Pines. Look for an open parking area on the left with a large pine tree in the center of it. A short hike up to the top of a small saddle and back to the west leads to a picturesque forest of pines and a series of wind-sculptured caves. This is an excellent short hike, a great place for kids to scramble on the rocks, and a nice picnic area.

2.0 Fremont Ridge Road. You can ride out this road approximately one mile before it drops steeply down into the Santa Ynez Valley. The ridge is relatively level, with rolling knolls and beautiful views over the valley. Please don't go below the dropoff point—beyond this is private property.

2.5 Painted Cave Road. Painted Cave is approximately a mile down this narrow road, which winds past Jane Fonda's Laurel Springs Ranch and the Painted Cave community, eventually leading back down to Highway 154. An excellent small book, "Guide to Painted Cave", by Travis Hudson, who was Curator of Anthropology at the Museum of Natural

History before his untimely death several years ago, can be purchased at most bookstores or at the Cielo Store.

3.7 Knapp's Castle turnoff. Snyder Trail leads down to Paradise Road (see trail description).

6.0 Arroyo Burro Road. A shooting area is just to the north side of the road where Arroyo Burro intersects with Camino Cielo, so be extremely careful should you decide to explore anywhere in this area. The historic Arroyo Burro Trail crosses here (see trail description).

8.0 La Cumbre Peak. At the 3,985' peak you'll not only have the best views in town but there are picnic tables for a pleasant afternoon's feast, and plenty of rocks for the kids (or you) to explore on the coast side of the crest. For those with a real sense of adventure, it is possible to work your way down the front side of the mountain, across a saddle, and up to the top of a lesser mountain called Cathedral Peak, a 300' spire which has a small trail register nestled in a mound of rocks.

9.0 Angostura Pass. From the pass, a dirt road leads 6 miles down to Gibraltar Dam. Two miles down this is the beginning of the Matias Potrero Trail, which leads across the back side of the mountains to Arroyo Burro Road (see trail descriptions).

10.0 Gibraltar Road. On the way down look for Gibraltar Rock, a large ice cube shaped boulder made of extremely resistant Matilija Sandstone, where you will usually be able to watch climbers testing their skill (and courage).

East Camino—Gibraltar Road to Blue Canyon

0.0 Intersection of Camino Cielo and Gibraltar roads

3.0 Cold Springs/Forbush Flats trailheads.

3.2 San Ysidro trailhead.

5.8 Romero Saddle. A dirt road from the saddle leads down into the upper Montecito foothills. This provides an excellent route either from town or back down into it (see description).

7.0 Start of the Divide Peak ORV trailhead. This leads for more than 10 miles along the last part of Camino Cielo (see trail description)

7.6 Escondido Creek. A picturesque picnic spot with a creek that usually runs year round.

9.0 Blue Canyon trailhead. The route leads down a strike canyon formed by the Santa Ynez Fault (see trail description).

Rock formations along West Camino Cielo provide a unique setting, especially at Lizard's Mouth, a favorite spot to watch the sun set.

WEST CAMINO CIELO

TRAIL INFORMATION: Length—10 miles Elevation Gain—700'
Difficulty—Moderate Topo—San Marcos Pass.

RECREATIONAL MAP SERIES: Map No. 4—Santa Barbara
Mountain Bike Routes—Trail #2

HIGHLIGHTS: The ride along the crest of West Camino Cielo
provides incredible views in either direction. Along the way you can
take short side trips to the Playground or Lizard's Mouth.

DIRECTIONS: Follow Highway 154 for 7 miles to San Marcos Pass.
Turn right on East Camino Cielo and park near the Cielo Store

From the Cielo Store, cross Highway 154, turn left on
Stagecoach Road, then almost immediately right on Kinevan
Road, which leads a little less than a mile down a small,
beautiful canyon to West Camino Cielo. It is surprising how
few people know this sylvan spot exists.

At West Camino Cielo, turn sharply to the right and follow
the winding road uphill out of the canyon. A half mile of
somewhat steep uphill brings you up onto the ridgeline. From
there you have a more gradual uphill for 4 miles to the end of
the pavement.

There are plenty of places to stop along the way to enjoy
the views and if you know where to find it, the trailhead
to the Playground is about 2.5 miles up West Camino. You will
know when you are nearing the end of the paved section
of the road when you find yourself immersed in more and
more sandstone outcroppings. There are lots of great rock
formations to explore, if you have time.

View from the top of West Camino Cielo, just before the turnoff to Tequepis Trail. Single track from here leads down to Lake Cachuma.

TEQUEPIS TRAIL

TRAIL INFORMATION: Length—Tequepis Trail—19 miles; 12 miles along West Camino Cielo, 7 miles down Tequepis Trail to intersection with Highway 154; elevation drop is 2,500' on the trail. Refugio Beach—17 miles along West Camino Cielo, 7 miles down to Refugio State Park. To Santa Ynez High School—17 miles along West Camino Cielo, 6 miles down to the high school   Difficulty—Moderately strenuous to strenuous   Topo—San Marcos Pass and Lake Cachuma.

RECREATIONAL MAP SERIES: Map No. 4—Santa Barbara Mountain Bike Routes—Trail #2

HIGHLIGHTS: The ride along the crest of West Camino Cielo provides incredible views in either direction. Much of the route is over rough dirt road, which lends a remote quality to the ride. Tequepis Trail is one of the most enjoyable single track sections in these mountains and provides a perfect way to end your trip.

DIRECTIONS: Follow Highway 154 for 7 miles to San Marcos Pass. Turn right on East Camino Cielo and park near the Cielo Store for an out-and-back ride. Or for one of the longer drives, turn left on West Camino Cielo and drive out to the end of the paved section to start (about 4.5 miles).

I've always enjoyed long day rides along mountain crests. The feeling of being on top of the world is wonderful and I love the openness. Any ride across the top of the Santa Ynez Mountains will provide this feeling, but this is especially true of the western end of the mountains.

Views of the Channel Islands and the Santa Ynez Valley are with you constantly, and the rough dirt road leading across the top is seldom traveled, providing a sense of solitude that is worth the effort.

From the Cielo Store, cross Highway 154, turn left on Stagecoach Road, then almost immediately right on Kinevan Road, which leads a mile down a small, beautiful canyon to West Camino Cielo. From there the road rises sharply for a half-mile, then turns to a more gradual uphill for 4.5 miles to the end of the pavement.

From this point, the distance out to Santa Ynez Peak is approximately 7 miles, providing you with the best of this part of the front country. Just after the start of the dirt, West Camino drops sharply to a saddle. From there it gradually makes its way for 6 miles to the high point, 4200' high Broadcast Peak. The uphill is steady, meaning that you won't find it as tough as you might think, and the views will help soften the effort.

While the way back is mostly downhill, there is one major drawback—at the end of the ride, when you'll probably be a bit tuckered, a 500' elevation gain awaits you, a series of switchbacks that lead back up to the paved section.

To make this a shorter out-and-back ride, consider driving along West Camino Cielo until the pavement ends, a distance of about 5 miles, and parking there.

Three distinct options are also available if you don't mind the effort involved in putting a shuttle together. Perhaps you can sweet talk a friend into helping out.

One possibility is to follow the ridge to Tequepis Trail which drops off the north side of the mountain just before the top of Broadcast Peak to a point near Lake Cachuma, providing almost 7 miles of excellent downhill single tracking. Or you might continue for several more miles (most of it is downhill) to Refugio Pass and from there either follow the pavement 7 miles south to Refugio Beach State Park or a similar distance down the north side to Santa Ynez High School. Each will provide you with an excellent day's trip.

The Tequepis Trail option is my favorite. The shuttle for it takes about a half hour. From San Marcos Pass continue on Highway 154 about 12 more miles to a side road just before the entrance to Lake Cachuma (look for a left turn lane and a sign which says "Camp Cielo"). You can park anywhere on this road where there is sufficient shoulder to do so safely. Return back to West Camino Cielo and drive out it to whatever point you'd like to start riding.

Though much of this ride is on paved and dirt road, the feeling that one gets is very special because of the sense of remoteness. To the south are views of the coast and the islands; to the north Lake Cachuma and the mountainous interior—much of it wilderness.

As you approach Broadcast Peak, look for the trail carefully. It leads to the right across a flat meadow, but it is hard to spot. The 7-mile ride down the trail is exhilarating and an excellent way to end the ride. As you approach the bottom of the trail (after a very steep 100 yard long drop the trail intersects a dirt road. Take the left fork, which leads down into the canyon and past several camps owned by private organizations. This route will take you to your car.

To continue on to Refugio Pass, ride over the broad left shoulder of Broadcast Peak (from which your favorite radio signals emanate) and on past a second high mountain, Santa Ynez Peak, then drop down for another 3 miles to the Pass. While I enjoy the ride down to the coast, the trip down the back side of Refugio Pass is wonderful, passing through lush canyon vegetation for 3.5 miles until it opens onto rolling hills and rustic looking ranches. I've spotted wild turkeys in this area. Another mile's ride brings you to the Santa Ynez River. Continue on Refugio Road to its intersection with Highway 154 where the high school is located.

Riding through oak forests and meadows near the bottom of Arroyo Burro Trail, just before its intersection with Arroyo Burro Road.

Looking down on Jameson Reservoir from a mile up the Franklin Trail. Below, in a delightful canyon, you'll find Alder Creek.

EAST CAMINO CIELO

TRAIL INFORMATION: Length—5 miles to FAA Radio Repeater;
8 miles to La Cumbre Peak   Difficulty—Moderately strenuous to
strenuous Topo—San Marcos Pass and Santa Barbara

HIGHLIGHTS: With views that equal those on West Camino Cielo,
the ride to La Cumbre Peak provides the feeling that you can see
almost forever. The ride is all on pavement, but does involve a great
deal of uphill riding. Shorter rides can be made, with side trips
either to Painted Cave or Knapp's Castle.

DIRECTIONS: Follow Highway 154 for 7 miles to San Marcos Pass.
Turn right on East Camino Cielo and park near the Cielo Store.
Please park along the road rather than in the store's parking area.

There are some riders who will look at you with scorn
etched in their eyes if you admit that you didn't ride up the
Pass before heading out across East Camino Cielo. To purists
this is a loop ride. Not me. I'm constantly amazed that anyone
would ride up Highway 154 when cars are buzzing by your
shoulder, many of them exceeding the speed limit on their race
over the Pass.

Instead, why not enjoy the pleasant company of the store
owners and other locals who happen by, have a cold drink or
get a last minute snack, and have a much safer ride by starting
from here? Besides, by making this an out-and-back ride
rather than a loop you can spend more time enjoying the many
treasures offered by the crest ride.

From the Cielo Store the road is almost level, undulating
through forests of oak and madrone, whose golden-orange
bark makes it look very much like manzanita. After a half-
mile, hopefully in which you've had a chance to stretch out

your leg muscles, the grind begins, first two steep switchbacks and then a long straightaway which is almost as steep.

If you can get by this section and still have a smile on your face, the rest will be a piece of cake. From this point, the uphill is mostly steady but not so hard on the legs. The best advice is to find a comfortable gear, get into your "all-day pace," and enjoy the beauty. The 5-mile point provides a convenient resting stop. Nearby is a radio repeater operated by the FAA which pilots use as a point of reference. La Cumbre Peak is another 3 miles and well worth the effort, though it will mean a 400' climb on the way back.

If you have time, take the short .75 mile side trip out to Knapp's Castle and spend a few minutes there before heading down to your car.

Bicyclist enjoying the Santa Ynez Valley views from Knapp's Castle.

Knapp's Castle is one of Santa Barbara's most historic ruins, one of four retreats built by George Owen Knapp in these mountains.

KNAPP'S CASTLE/LOOP

TRAIL INFORMATION: Length—3.5 miles to the ruins; 7.25 miles to Paradise Road on Snyder Trail; Complete Loop 14.5 miles Difficulty—Moderate to moderately strenuous depending on length Topo—San Marcos Pass (trail on this map shows only as a jeep road down to Lewis Falls)

RECREATIONAL MAP SERIES: Map No. 4—Santa Barbara Mountain Bike Routes—Trail #3

HIGHLIGHTS: The ride to Knapp's Castle provides a good combination of beautiful views and a great workout that ends at one of Santa Barbara's finest attractions, the historic ruins of Knapp's Castle. Synder Trail leads from the Castle down to the Santa Ynez Valley, providing a great loop trip that can be combined with a stop at Cold Springs Tavern.

DIRECTIONS: Follow Highway 154 for 7 miles to San Marcos Pass. Turn right on East Camino Cielo and park near the Cielo Store. Please park along the road rather than in the store's parking area.

One of the beauties of Cielo rides is the number of options available. Rides can be made as out-and-back excursions or as loops, with Snyder and Forbush trails and the Arroyo Burro and Angostura roads creating a variety of possibilities. You are limited only by the shape you are in.

Snyder Trail makes it possible to enjoy the historic beauty of Knapp's Castle, single track riding, and an afternoon of music at the Cold Springs Tavern, all in the space of a 14.5 mile loop.

To make the ride a bit easier, shuttle a second car to the Santa Barbara Ranger District office near Sage Hill beforehand. From Cielo Store pedal 3.5 miles (.75 beyond Painted

The view from the Castle is impressive, with country like this to be found just north of it, down in the Santa Ynez River canyon.

Cave Road) to a locked Forest Service gate on the left. This is the tough part of the ride.

From the gate an easy downhill ride to the Castle offers not only a glimpse of the past but the most spacious views of the Santa Ynez Valley possible. Please watch out for and be couteous to any hikers you might see. Several hundred yards before the ruins, Snyder Trail cuts off down and to the left, continuing 3 miles on a combination of dirt road and trail to Paradise Road.

The first 1.5 miles is actually Knapp's old road down built to provide access to his bath house, near Lewis Falls. After crossing under the power lines look on the left for the trail, which is marked by a small sign. The trail drops steeply downhill and is somewhat rutted. Unless your single track skills are proficient best is to walk your bike down this stretch. There is already too much rutting caused by riders using their brakes carelessly.

The remaining 1.5 miles consists of precipitous drops down grassy knolls and winding trail through oak forest. At the bottom head a locked gate announces your arrival at Paradise Road. Turn left, either to your shuttle car at Sage Hill or to continue along Paradise for 4 miles to Cold Springs Road. From there the uphill is steady for 4 miles to San Marcos Pass. At the halfway point up you'll find Cold Springs tavern, a welcome spot to rest.

ARROYO BURRO TRAIL

TRAIL INFORMATION: TRAIL INFORMATION: Length—7.75 (Cielo Store Loop 20 miles) TOTAL ELEVATION CHANGE: 2000' Difficulty—Moderately Strenuous   Topo—San Marcos Pass and Little Pine Mountain

RECREATIONAL MAP SERIES: Map No. 4—Santa Barbara Mountain Bike Routes—Trail #4

HIGHLIGHTS: Arroyo Burro Trail leads down to the Santa Ynez River to a point just above Lower Oso picnic area. Though there are some tough sections of single tracking (they can be easily walked) the route provides excellent riding down a picturesque canyon. The ride can be made either as a loop by continuing on west Paradise Road and eventually up past the Cold Springs Tavern to the Cielo Store or by returning back up the Arroyo Burro Road.

DIRECTIONS: Follow Highway 154 for 7 miles to San Marcos Pass. Turn right on East Camino Cielo and park near the Cielo Store. Please park along the road rather than in the store's parking area. To reach Arroyo Burro Road continue for 5.5 miles across East Camino Cielo to the saddle where it intersects with the paved road.

Beginning at the Cielo Store, Arroyo Burro Trail and/or Road provides another enjoyable possibility, though just a bit more strenuous than the Knapp's Loop. Not only is this an exhilarating bike ride, but it can be combined with a picnic or swim along the Santa Ynez River.

Ride (or drive) 5.5 miles from the Cielo Store to Arroyo Burro Saddle where the Arroyo Burro dirt road leads down the back side of the mountains into the Santa Ynez Valley. Several hundred yards down the road, Arroyo Burro Trail (difficult to see so watch closely for it) leads left down into a small drainage. Initially, the trail leads through chamise chaparral, then begins to drop somewhat steeply into the main canyon. Along some sections the trail is exposed, with long tumbles awaiting the rider who falls off the trail. Walk, don't ride, these parts.

Though the upper section of the trail is rarely used, there is a horse camp at the bottom. Ride slowly and enjoy the canyon's beauty, and please watch carefully for others on the trail.

Near the bottom at a trail split, turn right and cross the creek. This leads to an intersection with Arroyo Burro Road. Either head back uphill on the dirt road and back to your car or follow it downhill a mile to the river. A ride up the hard-packed river bottom leads to a number of swimming holes and potential picnic spots.

To complete your loop either ride 5 miles back up Arroyo Burro Road to your car or continue across the river and up to Paradise Road, turn left it and follow it to Cold Springs Road, the Tavern, and eventually the Cielo Store.

ANGOSTURA PASS

TRAIL INFORMATION: Length—11.5 miles TOTAL ELEVATION CHANGE: 2000' Difficulty—Moderate to Strenuous Topo—Santa Barbara and Little Pine Mountain

RECREATIONAL MAP SERIES: Map No. 4—Santa Barbara Mountain Bike Routes—Trail #6

HIGHLIGHTS: A well graded dirt road leads down to Gibraltar Dam from Angostura Pass, providing access to this part of the Santa Ynez River canyon. Matias Potrero Trail leads off the dirt road about 2 miles down, providing access to a number of loops in this area. Though a long climb back up the dirt road, this is a nice way to reach the swimming holes just above Red Rock.

DIRECTIONS: To reach Angostura Pass, follow Gibraltar Road 6.5 miles to East Camino Cielo, then turn left and drive another .7 miles to Angostura Pass. The dirt road is on the right, leading 6 miles down to Gibraltar Reservoir.

Angostura Pass Road provides entry into the upper Santa Ynez Valley from Santa Barbara, opening up a number of overnight possibilities, as well as the opportunity of combining trail and dirt road riding into a day's loop, complete with picnic, swimming, exploration or fishing spots.

While the dirt road's primary purpose is for servicing Gibraltar Reservoir, because it is locked and thus not open to the public, it provides an open and easily traveled path for those who would like to enjoy the beauty of a backcountry ride without the worry or bother of automobiles. For those who would like a strenuous hike, Matias Potrero and Devil's Canyon will suit your tastes as well.

The Matias Potrero Trail follows the Santa Ynez Fault, from Angostura Pass to Arroyo Burro Road. It begins a half mile from the top of Angostura Pass and is 6 miles long.

Initially, the road, which is smooth and well graded, winds gently downhill through the Pass then begins to cut across the back side of the Santa Ynez Mountains, in the process opening to expansive views of Little Pine and Big Pine Mountains. The ride through this section is leisurely and you can continue all the way down to the dam, though you'll have a lot of elevation gain on the way back.

Two miles down this road from Angostura Pass, Matias Potrero Trail leads steeply down and to the left. As it isn't marked with a sign you need to look for it carefully. This trail cuts across the north side of the Santa Ynez Mountains for 6 miles, eventually intersecting with Arroyo Burro Road. Along the way two connector trails lead down to the Santa Ynez River, one in Devil's Canyon and the other near Live Oak Picnic Area.

For a full day's adventure you might consider leaving a shuttle car at Live Oak or Red Rock, eventually dropping down to the Santa Ynez River via one of these connectors. A dip in the large pool at Live Oak, followed by a BBQ could provide the perfect touch following this ride.

It is also possible to continue across the entire length of the Matias Potrero Trail, then ride back up Arroyo Burro Road to Camino Cielo and east across it to your car (you'd better be in good shape!).

Devil's Canyon, which intersects with the Matias Potrero Trail 1.5 miles down the dirt road, leads to the Santa Ynez River near the base of Gibraltar Dam. To make this a loop ride, turn right at the Devil's Canyon intersection and continue 1.5 miles across the grassy slopes and through its picturesque narrows to the dam, then follow the dirt road back up to Angostura Pass, an 11 mile ride in total. Or continue down the river trail to one of the many swimming holes before heading back. If you have a shuttle awaiting you at Red Rock you can enjoy a full afternoon of splashing, sunning, and relaxing.

To complete the loop follow the dirt road back uphill 6 miles to Angostura Pass. Allow plenty of time to make it back up to the crest.

Rider enjoying the views at Forbush Flats, which is located directly in the Santa Ynez Fault. The campsite located here at the upper end of Gidney Creek provides a nice, easily reached overnight destination

FORBUSH FLATS

TRAIL INFORMATION: Length—Gibraltar Trail 3 miles; Santa Ynez River 3.5 miles; Cottam Camp 3.8 miles; Red Rock 12 miles TOTAL Elevation Loss—1075' to camp; 2000' to river   Difficulty—Moderate to strenuous depending on route chosen   Topo—Santa Barbara, Little Pine Mountain, Carpinteria, Hildreth Peak

RECREATIONAL MAP SERIES: Map No. 4—Santa Barbara Mountain Bike Routes—Trail #7

HIGHLIGHTS: The Forbush Trail provides access to the entire upper Santa Ynez River canyon as well as routes into the Red Rock and Lower Oso area. The trail provides excellent single track and the possibility of an overnight trip at either Forbush Flats or a number of other spots. With a shuttle, you can ride to Lower Oso, or make a long loop via Blue Canyon.

DIRECTIONS: To reach Forbush Trail follow Gibraltar Road 6.5 miles to East Camino Cielo, then turn right and drive another 3.75 miles to the trailhead, which is opposite the end of Cold Springs Trail. These trails are at a saddle just after a downhill section of road. A trail sign on the left and a cement water tank on the right side of the road should make it easy to spot.

   The Forbush Trail (a continuation of the Cold Springs Trail) offers access to a number of parts of the upper Santa Ynez Valley and day loops, shuttle trips, or overnighters depending on the type of arrangements you make.

   Originally it was one of the main thoroughfares into the backcountry, leading from Montecito through the upper part of the Santa Ynez drainage, along Mono Creek, and over a window in the San Rafael range known as the *Puerto Suelo* to Santa Barbara Canyon and the Cuyama Valley.

Due to its historical importance, the Cold Springs Trail feeds into the entire upper and lower Santa Ynez Recreation Areas. By bicycle, the number of loop or shuttle possibilities are almost unlimited. With appropriate gear it would even be possible to ride within 10 miles of Santa Maria, the upper end of the Cuyama Valley or within a few miles of Ojai and not once cross a paved road.

The first 1.5 miles of the trail leads through chaparral to Forbush Flat, dropping a thousand feet in elevation (meaning that you won't want to go back up the trail). The camp is pleasant, well shaded and at the foot of Gidney Creek, which often flows year round, though not always. Nearby is a small meadow, complete with an aging apple orchard, courtesy of Fred Forbush, who built a cabin there about 1910.

The camp is situated on top of the Santa Ynez Fault, which cuts directly through it, forming the crease along which Gidney Creek flows. Due to the uplifting which has occurred here, numerous layers of bedrock rich in fossil life are exposed here, making this an amateur geologist's paradise.

A trail intersection lies just north of the meadow. The main trail continues north, up over a 50' high ridge and then down another 1000' in elevation loss over 1.5 miles to the Santa Ynez River. Along the way are more fossils and a pool or two for refreshment. Near the bottom of the trail you'll find the end of Gibraltar Trail which leads to Gibraltar Reservoir and eventually Red Rock (this makes a great ride if you have a shuttle set up).

From the river there are a number of possibilities. You can cross the river and follow the Mono Trail to Mono Debris Dam, and then return on Pendola Road (a long, long loop ride). You can also stay on the south side of the river and head upstream. After a short hike through willow thickets the river bottom opens up and a dirt road leads upstream to Blue Canyon. From here you can cross the river and continue over to the Pendola Road near P-Bar Flats or head up Blue Canyon to Cottam Camp and then up the Blue Canyon trail.

From Forbush Flats, the right trail leads 2 miles east down through the Santa Ynez Fault and rugged chaparral to Cottam Camp which is located at the bottom end of Blue Canyon. From Cottam either follow this trail downstream from Cottam Camp to the Santa Ynez River, P-Bar Flats and the Pendola Road, or pedal up Blue Canyon (see Blue Canyon description).

ROMERO ROAD

RIDE INFORMATION: Distance—5 miles Elevation Gain—2175'
Difficulty—Moderate to strenuous   Topo—Carpinteria

RECREATIONAL MAP SERIES: Map No. 4—Santa Barbara
Mountain Bike Routes—Trail #1

HIGHLIGHTS: This beautiful route to the top of the mountains is
the only trail I recommend riding in the Front Country—and it isn't
even a trail. Rather, it is the remains of a historic dirt road, a
reminder of what Santa Barbara's mountain roads were once like.
After 1978 it was closed to public automobile travel after heavy
rainstorms caused huge slides across it. What it provides is mountain
bike access to the backcountry.

DIRECTIONS: From Highway 101 take the Sheffield Drive exit.
Follow it 1.5 miles to East Valley Road. Turn left, then almost
immediately to the right on Romero Canyon Road and continue
another 1.5 miles to Bella Vista and turn right on it. The trailhead
is about .3 miles. You find a locked red steel gate marking the trail's
beginning.

There is no better place to go than Romero Road to find a
bike ride that combines scenery and getting in shape. It also
provides a bicycle route into and out of the upper Santa Ynez
Valley, allowing a number of shuttle options or opportunities
for weekend overnight trips from Santa Barbara. What other
cities in Southern California offer such a possibility for
mountain bikers?

Romero Road at one time was a public road but it has been
closed since the 1970s and subsequently nature has retaken
much of it, returning it more to the status of trail than road.
It winds moderately uphill for 4.5 miles to the crest and offers

excellent views and exciting riding due to ample exposures of Coldwater and Matilija sandstone. This makes the ride a trials adventure, though as more and more people ride it the trail is becoming smoother and smoother.

From the locked gate follow a dirt road straight up a grade for a half mile. This part isn't too steep but it is loose and somewhat rutted, making you wonder what you've gotten yourself into. But don't worry, the best is ahead. In a bit the road levels out and then splits, the left turn a road accessing the power lines. Curve to the right and cross Romero Creek. Beyond here the road becomes overgrown as it starts to rise and is now a trail. For the next mile it gradually curves back to the left and around a large peak formed from Matilija Sandstone. There are lots of places to stop for views of Montecito, and as you curve further around, of Toro Canyon.

Eventually you come to a saddle and you continue through it which takes you back into the Romero drainage. The next 1.5 miles of riding are wonderful as it makes a complete circle of the drainage. The road is almost completely level. The road is shale and crumbles easily, making the path smooth, which is nice after the rocky first mile. At a fork of Romero Creek a small creek bubbles up and it is a great place to splash water over your (probably) sweat-drenched face. Another half mile brings you to an intersection with Romero Trail. It is 1.5 miles beyond this point to Romero Saddle.

With a bit of judicious planning you can continue on into the backcountry on one of the trails leading down to the Santa Ynez River. My personal favorite is the Cold Springs Trail. From Romero Saddle, this trail is 2.8 miles west. I drop down it, stop for a few minutes at Forbush Flats, then continue on down to the Gibraltar Trail and then past the Sunbird Mine to Red Rock, where I have a shuttle car waiting for me.

Another great ride can be made by continuing even further west on Camino Cielo to Angostura Pass and then down it to Matias Potrero Trail. It can take you either to Red Rock or Live Oak picnic area. Or you are planning on spending a weekend in the upper Santa Ynez River canyon, why not ride over via the Romero roadway and meet your friends (if they'll do this for you they are true, true friends) at your campsite?

A long day's loop ride can also be done by riding back down Gibraltar Road. To reach it from Romero Saddle, turn left and ride 5.8 miles west on Camino Cielo. There is a bit of elevation gain out of Romero Saddle but after a half mile Camino Cielo is almost completely level all the way to Gibraltar Road. It's all downhill from there.

Because the upper half of the Cold Springs Trail is rarely used, one possible way to get in a small amount of single tracking is to take it down to the power line road, turn left, and continue down it into Hot Springs Canyon then back through Montecito to your car. The upper Cold Springs trailhead is 2.8 miles from Romero Saddle and next to a large cement water tank (opposite the Forbush Flats trailhead).

DIVIDE PEAK

TRAIL INFORMATION: Length—Franklin Loop 18 miles; Divide Peak Loop 24.5 miles   Difficulty—Strenuous to Hard Core   Topo—Carpinteria and White Ledge Peak

RECREATIONAL MAP SERIES: Map No. 4—Santa Barbara Mountain Bike Routes—Trail #9

HIGHLIGHTS: The Divide Peak route leads across the furthermost east part of Camino Cielo, with spectacular views out over the Carpinteria Valley and the upper Santa Ynez River drainage. The route involves some steep uphills but they are worth it. If you are adventurous you can take the Franklin Trail down to Jameson Reservoir for a long day's loop.

DIRECTIONS: To reach the Divide Peak turnout, follow Gibraltar Road 6.5 miles to East Camino Cielo, then turn right. After 5.8 miles of pavement, the road turns to dirt just beyond Romero Saddle. The turnout, a large parking area set aside for motorcyclists, is approximately 1.2 miles down from the Saddle.

This route is absolutely my favorite crest ride, offering a great day's ride though accompanied by an occasional push. The ridge is sharp, steeply tilted upward, forming the highest part of the 50-mile length of the Santa Ynez Mountains, rising almost a mile above the coastline. The views are equally sharp and most of what is on display is above the Santa Barbara haze (some would call it smog). For both island views and backcountry panoramas the Divide Peak Jeep Trail is in a class by itself.

It is frustrating as well, somewhat spoiled by the occasional ORV user you may see. While many of them are polite, some roar by at full speed and volume) shattering the peaceful nature of this part of the mountain wall. It is hard to understand that this type of use can be tolerated, but then hikers often wonder the same thing about mountain bikers.

The first 3 miles of riding meanders gently uphill through the chaparral to Toro Saddle, allowing ample time to stretch leg and arm muscles. The Saddle provides the first of many view spots, and is a great place to stop if only interested in a short day's ride.

Thereafter, the road steepens, paralleling the coast for .25 miles then turning left and sharply uphill, leading to a 4000' crest which yo yos up and down for 10 miles to Divide Peak. For the next five miles the road, now a 4-wheel route, undulates over a series of knolls, which means short, gnarly uphills (on which you may have to push) and exhilarating downhills.

Approximately 5 miles east of Toro Saddle, Franklin Trail crosses over the crest. This trail isn't marked and is difficult to find. Look for a saddle with a power line leading down in the canyon. The trail leads at an angle back to the left and directly under the power line.

Just beyond the saddle, the jeepway turns slightly to the right and steeply up, then to the left. Several rock ledges cut across the jeepway, making it almost impossible to ride up the road. These should help you find the trail. Better yet, bring the topos along.

Because the Franklin Trail is rarely maintained it is somewhat overgrown, especially near the top. It also contains many switchbacks, but the slowness this produces provides more time to enjoy the canyon beauty. This area has the feel of real wildness (which you'll find to be the case if you have a problem).

A mile down the trail you'll find a delightful overnight spot, Alder Camp, which is perfect for an overnight. It is amazing how quickly you can go in the space of a few moments from views of heavily traveled Highway 101 and tract homes to a place such as Alder Camp, where you'll feel like you are in the middle of nowhere. In reality, however, you aren't that isolated. A mile further the trail ends at Jameson Reservoir, Montecito's water supply, where you can get help if needed.

From there the ride continues 3 miles downhill to Juncal Camp, then 4 miles back up to your starting point. Be sure to turn left and go back up Pendola Road towards Romero Saddle. At Jameson Reservoir it is also possible to turn right and ride into the upper end of the Santa Ynez River drainage. This leads to a small camp called Upper Santa Ynez and Murietta Divide which leads to Matilija Hot Springs and upper Ojai Valley (see Murietta Divide/Pendola Loop trail description).

The longer loop continues along the crest for an additional 5 miles, with the route getting increasingly rocky and difficult to negotiate. Near the end it rises sharply uphill for 700' to Divide Peak. While the view is spectacular, continuing further is for the hard core who are either in great shape or don't care what they'll feel like by the day's end.

From Divide Peak, Monte Arido Trail leads very steeply downhill for 1 mile to Murietta Divide (this is a push, not ride section). From there it is possible to ride east into Matilija Canyon and eventually to Ojai, or west 3 miles downhill to Jameson Reservoir. Upper Santa Ynez Camp is a half-mile west of the divide and has a dependable supply of water.

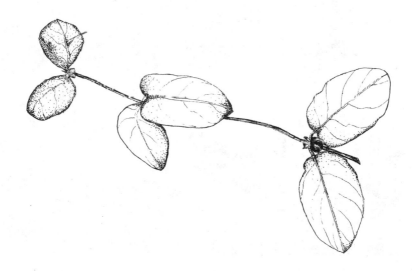

BLUE CANYON

TRAIL INFORMATION: Length— Short Loop 13 miles; Long Loop
17.5 miles Elevation Loss—800' Difficulty—Moderate to Strenuous
Topo—Carpinteria, Hildreth Peak and Little Pine Mountain

RECREATIONAL MAP SERIES: Map No. 4—Santa Barbara
Mountain Bike Routes—Trail #8

HIGHLIGHTS: Blue Canyon provides excellent single track riding
as well as a beautiful small canyon. There are several camps if you
would like to make an overnight ride, as well as a number of loop
possibilites, either via Mono Debris Dam or just along the Pendola
Road. With a shuttle, you can ride all the way to Lower Oso.

DIRECTIONS: To reach Blue Canyon Trail, follow Gibraltar Road
6.5 miles to East Camino Cielo, then turn right. After 5.8 miles of
pavement, the road turns to dirt just beyond Romero Saddle.
Continue 3.8 miles further on this rather rough dirt road to the
trailhead (marked by a sign) at a prominent saddle which marks the
beginning of Blue Canyon.

Blue Canyon, named for the bluish-green serpentine formations exposed along its entire length, can be used either for
day loop rides or as part of an overnight trip beginning from
Santa Barbara via Romero Road.

The route parallels a small stream for 5.5 miles, combining
canyon vegetation and an oak woodland setting along the way
before finally opening into a large meadow in which Cottam
Camp is situated. The trail crosses the creek several times and
in some places the scrub oak is overgrown, but the single
tracking for the most part is enjoyable, especially the upper
half, which is a trials rider's paradise.

Both Upper Blue Canyon Camp (at 1.5 miles) and Blue Canyon Camp (at 4.2 miles) are small but serviceable, while Cottam is under the shelter of several large oaks at the edge of several acres of meadow. Below Cottam, the trail is slightly hidden. Look for it across and 40 yards upstream from camp. It is .7 miles to the Santa Ynez River where you will come to a dirt road.

For the shorter loop turn to the right and continue on the road across the Santa Ynez River for .8 miles to Pendola Road and P-Bar Flats. If you have time, take a detour up to the Pendola Hot Springs. It is 2.5 miles, but the ride is almost level from Pendola Station up Agua Caliente Canyon to the hot springs and the soak in the hot tub will be worth it. The return to the trailhead via Pendola Road is 6 miles.

For the longer loop turn left and follow the dirt road down the left side of the river for 1.2 miles and work your way along an overgrown trail composed of willow and cottonwood thickets .3 mile to the base of the Cold Springs Trail. Follow it downstream .1 mile and cross the river. On the other side it becomes the Mono Trail, which leads .5 mile down the north side to Mono Creek. The 1.5 mile ride up it winds through clusters of cottonwood and more willow, which are so thick as to form a tunnel of greenery. The trail ends at Mono Camp, an open camp situated in a scattering of huge oak trees near the base of Mono Debris Dam. To complete the loop follow Pendola Road 8 miles back to the trailhead.

Lower Santa Ynez River Canyon

When the river rises and the gate across the Santa Ynez riverbed near Los Prietos Boy's Camp is closed, the canyon becomes quiet. A few mountain bikers haul their bikes across the river and pedal towards Upper Oso or Red Rock, thankful they'll have the area to themselves for a day or two until the river comes down. A family or two ford the river as well, still intent on having a picnic, whether they can drive across or not. Even the inner tubers are out, getting ready for a float down to Sage Hill Campground.

Otherwise, there is only the quiet sound of nature—the sway of willow and cattail, the chattering of blackbirds, and whoosh-whoosh of a light breeze. On my bike, I ride up the canyon beyond Lower Oso, cuttting up and across the left side of the canyon, then coasting down to Falls picnic area and a second river crossing. From here the next three miles are almost level.

The road undulates through the upper canyon, walls narrowing to form steep, shaly slopes and vertical layers of sandstone. Beyond the second crossing I find Santa Ynez campground deserted. A half-mile later I see the rough trail leading down to the left and across the river to Camuesa Connector and just beyond that, on the right, a locked gate that marks the beginning of a spur that climbs up onto the north slope of the Santa Ynez Mountains, intersecting with Matias Potrero Trail a mile later.

A quarter mile beyond the locked gate the road crosses, then recrosses, the river in the span of several hundred yards.

A beautiful picnic area—Live Oak—is in between the two crossings, at an elbow in the river. Large oaks shelter the tables and cooking areas. A long, deep pool lies just below the elbow, resting against the edge of a long sandstone cliff that makes this spot particularly inviting.

The next mile is my favorite, a distance in which the river cuts across the road 3 times. The canyon is sharp and twisty, with cottonwoods and sycamore defining the river's edge. The pools are abundant, and perfect in the summer months. If it weren't for the paved road, this would be wild country. Still, it has a rustic and rugged quality about it.

Just beyond this I come to a last pool with a beach area almost 50 yards long. This pool, like Live Oak, rests against a sandstone ledge. The stone is tilted at an angle of about 60 degrees and footsteps cut in the rock lead up to a series of ledges which create jumping off points 10-to-15 feet above the water. In the summer this is the most popular place to hang out anywhere along the river.

Almost abruptly the road ends in a large, open dirt parking area that is covered by huge oaks. This marks the end of the drive and the beginning of a level half-mile walk to Red Rock, perhaps the most beautiful pool to be found anywhere along the Santa Ynez River.

If you are a botanist or a geologist, this is a country that must speak to you eloquently. Though not in words, the land speaks. Knowing a little you can discover a lot. Prior to the mid-1800s it was a land that was defined on nature's terms—hot, parched summers; a fall season filled with acorns bursting forth from huge oaks; a deep, roaring river, often overflowing its banks and replenishing meadows with top soil in the winter; and the greens and pastels of wildflowers and tall grasses in the springtime—a land that evolved to the beat of a different and far, far slower drummer.

Santa Barbara Ranger District

You'll find the district office located at the Los Prietos Ranger Station on Paradise Road, 4 miles east of Highway

154. The office is open from 8am-5pm Monday through Friday and most Saturdays throughout the summer. For information you can write (Los Prietos Ranger Station, Star Route, Santa Barbara, CA 93105 or call (805/967-3481).

The district is comprised of approximately 232,000 acres which includes the Santa Ynez Mountains, most of the upper Santa Ynez River drainage, and a portion of the San Rafael Wilderness. Entry into some areas may be prohibited during periods of high fire danger.

Picnicking

Four picnic areas are located along the river: White Rock; Lower Oso; Falls; and Live Oak. White Rock is located along Paradise Road about 3 miles from the Highway 154 turnoff. Lower Oso is immediately after the first river crossing. Falls picnic area is just before the second river crossing and Live Oak is just after the third crossing. All have tables, B-B-Q pits and restroom facilities.

Camping

Five family campgrounds are located in the Canyon— Fremont, Paradise, Los Prietos, Upper Oso, and Santa Ynez— and one group campground, Sage Hill, which is located just behind the Ranger Station.

Fremont, Paradise, and Los Prietos can be found along Paradise Road between Highway 154 and the Ranger Station. Upper Oso is located a mile up a spur road leading north just opposite Lower Oso picnic area. Santa Ynez Camp is in the upper canyon, just beyond Falls picnic area and after the second river crossing.

All have paved roads, piped water, B-B-Q pits, tables, trash bins, and restrooms. While some of them have extralong parking areas suitable for trailers, none have hookups. The fee per night is $5 per site. Each site allows up to 8 people and 2 cars.

Sage Hill has 5 group campsites, with each capable of handling from 25-50 people. Each is equipped with a centralized cooking and eating area, a group B-B-Q pit, a fire pit, water faucets, and flush toilets. Corrals are available for those with horses. The fee per night is $25 per site. Reservations can be made by contacting the Los Prietos Ranger Station (805/ 967-3481) up to 90 days in advance. A $10 non-refundable deposit is required.

With the exception of Sage Hill, all camps are on a first-come, first-serve basis. Length of stay is limited to 14 days and the designated "Quiet Time" is from 10pm through 6am. Pets are required by law to be on a leash.

Access to the canyon—which includes the river and most picnic areas—is open from 6am to 8pm. The Live Oak picnic area and all general canyon use beyond Santa Ynez Campground closes at 8pm.

Campfires, B-B-Q's, and fuel stoves are allowed only in the facilities provided at designated sites either at campgrounds or day use areas. Camping is permitted only in campgrounds. No hunting or shooting is allowed in the Recreation Area.

The Ride To Little Pine

The dirt road to the top of Little Pine Mountain rises inexorably, a dozen switchbacks, then a long climb up an extended ridge brings us to its face, a sheer thousand foot escarpment known as the Chalk Bluffs. They are composed of cream-colored shales laid down 20 million years ago, long before pressures along the nearby San Andreas Fault pushed them skyward.

Pedaling steadily, we continue up more switchbacks which take us around the east side of the mountain. At a saddle at the top of the last long push we stop for a rest, a drink of water, and a moment to absorb the quiet beauty of the back country and island views on the distant horizon.

For me, this is what mountain biking is all about: the experience of nature firsthand; the opportunity to discover new places with friends; the excitement and adventure of riding; moments like this to get away from the pressures and over-regulation of urban life.

Though not without effort, the rest of the trip is equally pleasurable: five miles of gentle trail down into Buckhorn Canyon rolling silently along, listening to the sound of wren and the small creek, thoroughly enjoying the feeling of moving deep into the heart of these mountains; four miles along a larger creek where we stop to swim and have lunch; then on dirt road once more, ten miles of gradual uphill through a narrow, twisting canyon back to the Little Pine Road, and from there five more steeply downhill to the trailhead at Upper Oso Campground. In all we traveled thirty-three miles on our bikes that day. It was not only great physical exercise, but each of us was revitalized by the contact with the back country experience. Nor would it have been possible on anything but a mountain bike.

The Rides Awaiting You

There are many such places like this awaiting you in the Santa Ynez Valley and the mountains diectly behind Santa Barbara, trips you can take by bike which can last from several hours to several days. You can stay entirely on roads or trails, or put together a combination of both to create a variety of loops. Access to them is rarely more than a half hour to forty-five minute car ride from Santa Barbara. You are limited only by your imagination, and perhaps, by the shape you are in.

Most of the land on either side of the upper Santa Ynez Valley is mountainous. Situated near the edge of two gigantic tectonic plates the land has been caught as if in a vise and crumpled, causing the creation of a series of east-west trending ranges. North of the Santa Ynez Valley you'll find the San Rafael Mountains, a range which averages 5000-6000 feet in elevation and contains some of the finest stands of pine forest in the county.

It has also been the home of the California condor in the past, and hopefully will be in the future, if the recovery program is successful in restoring them to this habitat. Just recently, the first two captive bred birds were released into the Ventura backcountry. The pair, a male named Chocuyens, and the female, Xewe, were brought to the remote site in October, 1991 to begin acclimatizing to their new environment. They were released for the first time on January 14, 1992.

Xewe is a Chumash word meaning "to cast a shadow." Until the mid-1980s, when the last remaining wild condor was captured to protect it, these vultures cast many a giant shadow over this country, soaring effortlessly and gracefully on the updrafts created by the mountainous country. The mother of Xewe was the last Condor captured in 1987.

Getting to Paradise

Directions for each of the rides begin from the Lower Oso picnic area, which is at the beginning of the lower canyon section. It is located on Paradise Road, 5 miles east of Highway 154. Look for it just after the first river crossing at Los Prietos Boy's Camp.

LOWER OSO/UPPER OSO

TRAIL INFORMATION: Distance—2 miles Elevation Gain— 200'
Difficulty— Easy Topo—San Marcos Pass

HIGHLIGHTS: This is a short trail, which follows the left side of the
road leading to Upper Oso and provides either a short and scenic
day ride or a way to and from Upper Oso without having to ride on
the road.

DIRECTIONS: From Lower Oso picnic area, take the road leading
to Upper Oso and follow it several hundred yards. Just after
crossing a bridge look for the trail, which leads left and across a
small creek.

This short trail is a mile in length and provides an excellent
warmup before tackling the big one—the road to Little Pine.
The trail twists and winds its way through a series of meadows
and a few chaparral sections to the lower end of the camp at
Upper Oso. For beginners, it provides a good introduction to
what single track riding is like.

If you would like to extend your bike ride, continue on past
the locked Forest Service gate into the narrow upper canyon.
This is composed of Matilija Sandstone, the same rock found
at the top of La Cumbre Peak. Three-fourths mile up through
the narrows you will come to the beginning of the Santa Cruz
Trail. The first mile of this trail is heavily used by hikers and
equestrian groups and I would recommend you continue on
the road rather than riding up the trail.

Either return on the road or ride back down the trail to
Lower Oso.

ARROYO BURRO ROAD

TRAIL INFORMATION: Distance—5 miles one way   Elevation Gain—2035' Difficulty—Moderate to Strenuous depending on how far you go   Topo—San Marcos Pass and Little Pine Mountain

RECREATIONAL MAP SERIES: Map No. 4—Santa Barbara Mountain Bike Routes—Trail #4

HIGHLIGHTS: Arroyo Burro Road winds its way somewhat steeply up a ridge to the crest of the Santa Ynez Mountains. In the canyon, to the right of the road, Arroyo Burro Trail is located, making it possible to ride the road up and take the trail back down. A mile uphill is the turnoff to Matias Potrero and beyond that are wonderful views of the valley, though purchased through a somewhat strenuous effort.

DIRECTIONS: From Lower Oso ride .8 miles east on Paradise Road to the White Oaks turnoff. Turn right on it and drop down across the river to the start of Arroyo Burro Road.

At first the dirt road leads up a small canyon and the riding doesn't seem too tough, but shortly afterwards it turns left and begins to meander back and forth up a large ridge towards the crest. A mile from the river, in a turnout on the right, you'll find the lower end of Arroyo Burro Trail. You can stash your bikes here and take a pleasant hike or it is also possible to go west across the creek and into what was once Rancho Oso (now a park for motor home buffs). A paved road leads through the ranch and back to Paradise Road near the Boy's Camp. Lower Oso is a quarter mile to the right.

About 2.8 miles from the river Matias Potrero Trail leads off to the right. Beyond this the road rises steadily uphill for another 2 miles to the crest. Just before a shooting area located there, Arroyo Burro Trail leads off to the right. One of Santa Barbara's most historic trails, it was probably built by the Chumash who used it as a trading route to interior villages.

The trail winds through chamise chaparral at first then begins to drop steeply down into a narrow, rocky canyon, which is shaded and filled with lush riparian vegetation and a cool creek which runs year round except in extremely dry years. You can follow the trail back down (see Crest trail description) or return via the road.

For those who are truly hard core, turn east on Camino Cielo and ride over La Cumbre Peak to Angostura Pass and the dirt road back down into the Santa Ynez Valley either on Matias Potrero Trail or via the Santa Ynez River.

MATIAS POTRERO

TRAIL INFORMATION: Distance—Short Loop 10.5 miles; Long Loop 18 miles Elevation Gain— Short Loop 800'; Long Loop 1200' Difficulty—Moderate to Moderately Strenuous Topo—San Marcos Pass and Little Pine Mountain

RECREATIONAL MAP SERIES: Map No. 4—Santa Barbara Mountain Bike Routes—Trail #5

HIGHLIGHTS: This trail leads across the north side of the Santa Ynez Mountains through open fields of grass and a series of ridges from Arroyo Burro Road to Gibraltar Dam. With the exception of the ups and downs of the ridgelines, surprisingly the trail is almost level, and high enough from the valley floor to provide scenic views of the canyon and the San Rafeal Mountains. You'll find great trials sections and if you continue across to Devil's Canyon, a challenging last mile. On the way back you can stop along the river for a refreshing dip in one of the many pools.

DIRECTIONS: The loop begins from the parking area at Lower Oso picnic area. From the picnic area ride .8 miles to the White Oaks turnoff. Turn right on it and go down across the river to the start of Arroyo Burro Road. Ride up the road 2.8 miles to the Matias Potrero trailhead. It is marked by a small sign and is just beyond a large, open grass-covered saddle.

Matias Potrero Trail was once a dirt road servicing power lines that were constructed in the 1960s. Now it is overgrown enough to have become a trail. It follows the Santa Ynez Fault along the lower north slope of the Santa Ynez Mountains. Bluish-green serpentine, upthrust along the fault, has created a soil which supports a swath of grassy slopes and potreros, making this a picturesque area. It also is a favorite area for ticks so check often for them.

The trail meanders across a series of canyons and ridges for 2.5 miles to an intersection just before Matias Potrero Camp. To complete the short loop turn left and ride downhill 1 mile to the road (near Live Oak picnic area), then 3.3 miles left and back to the parking area.

For the longer loop continue on the trail. Not too far along Matias Potrero Camp is located, a small site in the vee of a small canyon. Look for a high trail a few yards beyond the trail sign, rather than taking the one which heads down to Matias Potrero Camp. You can go through the camp but the trail is pretty steep on the other side of it.

The high trail cuts around and above the camp, thus avoiding the drop and climb. Follow the high trail two miles further east. At this point you'll find a trail intersection. While Matias Potrero heads up to Angostura Pass, the trail is too steep to ride. You'll find yourself pushing quite a bit of the way. The left fork leads down into Devil's Canyon and 1.5 miles of slightly more difficult riding to Gibraltar Dam.

The ride back from there along the Santa Ynez River to the Lower Oso parking area is 8 miles in length.

Looking out across the Santa Ynez Valley from the Matias Potrero Trail. In the springtime, the grasses here are prime tick country.

LITTLE PINE

TRAIL INFORMATION: Distance—20 miles   Elevation Gain—
3300' Difficulty—Strenuous Topo—San Marcos Pass and Little
Pine Mountain

RECREATIONAL MAP SERIES: Map No. 4—Santa Barbara
Mountain Bike Routes—Trail #10

HIGHLIGHTS: This is the premier ride in the upper Santa Ynez
Valley. Incredible views, secluded stands of pine atop Little Pine
Mountain, and an exhilarating ride back down make this one of the
most worthwhile rides in Santa Barbara County. However, its 3400'
elevation gain demands that you be in pretty good physical shape
to enjoy it all the way up. Along the way you will find a host of trails
and connector roads, which provide numerous loop possibilities and
the best, most challenging riding anywhere in Santa Barbara
County.

DIRECTIONS: From Lower Oso picnic area, turn left and follow the
spur road leading a mile to Upper Oso.

CAUTION: The Buckhorn Road is open to ORV use. You should be
alert for their presence. Please be extremely cautious and on the
lookout for horse riders. The Santa Cruz Trail is used extensively
by equestrian groups. Assume a rider is just around each corner. If
necessary, dismount from your bike and ask the horse rider what
he/she would like you to do.

A dirt road—the Buckhorn Road—leads to the top of Little
Pine. The first .75 mile leads through the shaded beauty of Oso
Canyon, gradually gaining elevation and providing an easy
way to stretch out you legs. The canyon walls are narrow,
looming almost directly overhead, the formation composed of
Matilija Sandstone, the same as at the top of La Cumbre Peak.

*Just starting down the Santa Cruz Trail from Alexander Saddle,
which is a half mile from the crest of Little Pine Mountain.*

At the three-quarter mile mark, Santa Cruz Trail leads off to the left. From here the road ascends rapidly up a series of switchbacks. Though only a mile in length, they never seem to end. Beyond here the road cuts up and around the left side of a large peak, providing shade for the next mile, to a large open grass meadow where Camuesa Connector trail begins.

From here the route follows a long ridgeline past the Old Mine Road, then goes west around another peak to its intersection with Camuesa Road, which marks the halfway point to Little Pine Mountain.

Fortunately the next mile is almost level, at one place dropping down several hundred feet to a small saddle. At this point the crux of the ride begins as the road begins to rise steeply again. Several switchbacks lead to the Chalk Bluffs and from there you've got a half-mile of effort ahead of you— a tortuous half mile. The road is more a series of staircases than a steady uphill grind, with short almost level sections followed by steep little hills.

Around the corner a treat awaits you. The road is level for a half mile and then begins to wind up through a series of gradual climbs over the eastern shoulder of Little Pine that give your aching legs a needed rest. Monterey Shale dominates this part of the mountain, as well as the mountain crest. It weathers to a rich, loamy soil that supports an abundance of grass and huge fields of golden poppies, lupine, goldfields, cream cups and other wildflowers in the springtime.

On the top of the shoulder, Buckhorn Trail leads off to the right. A mile further (a last steep section), a water tank marks the turnoff that leads to the top of the mountain. Though it is 2 miles long, the road is gradual, an easy climb after what you've already encountered, at first through manzanita forests, then near the top thick clusters of pines.

The road leads down into Happy Hollow, a large depression that seems almost like the inner core of an extinct volcano, though the pine forests that surround the small camp area make it seem like a piece of heaven. Just to the south a short climb brings you to the summit of Little Pine, a rounded, grass-covered mound that opens onto fabulous views of the entire Santa Ynez Valley complex, the Santa Ynez Mountains, and beyond them the Channel Islands. This view alone makes the ride a rewarding one.

From here, a short, very steep spur trail leads down to a saddle where you will find the Santa Cruz Trail. The route back down is 7 miles of incredible single tracking, eventually coming back out on Buckhorn Road .75 miles from Upper Oso camp.

The safest return route is via the road and eliminates any conflicts with hikers or horseback riders. If you take the road back you might consider one of the connector trails on your return trip, rather than following the dirt road all the way. Camuesa Connector and the Old Mine Road both provide excellent ways to finish out the ride.

CAMUESA CONNECTOR

TRAIL INFORMATION: Distance—12 miles   Difficulty—
Moderate   Topo—San Marcos Pass and Little Pine Mountain
(Camuesa Connector Trail not on the map)

RECREATIONAL MAP SERIES: Map No. 4—Santa Barbara
Mountain Bike Routes—Trail #11

HIGHLIGHTS: This is an excellent morning or afternoon ride
which takes no more than 3 hours to complete, though more may be
added either by picnicking along the way or stopping at Live Oak
picnic area near the trail's end, where you'll find a great swimming
hole waiting for you. The single track on Camuesa Connector is the
best 3-mile section found anywhere in the valley.

DIRECTIONS: From Upper Oso ride up Buckhorn Road (same
route as for Little Pine) for 3.2 miles to the Camuesa Connector
trailhead. It is marked by a sign which is easily spotted, at the edge
of a large meadow. Turn right and at first ride down a dirt road
which goes through the meadow. At the point where the road drops
down to a low point and then seems to head up an extremely steep
hill, look to the left for the trail. It winds up a small drainage
towards a small saddle which can be seen in the distance.

CAUTION: The Buckhorn Road is open to ORV use. You should be
alert for their presence. Please be extremely cautious and on the
lookout for horse riders. The area is used extensively by equestrian
groups. Assume a rider is just around each corner. If necessary,
dismount from your bike and ask the horse rider what he/she would
like you to do.

For single tracking, there is none better to be found than
on the Camuesa Connector, which is cut along a fault line that
creates a series of saddles leading southeast and eventually to
the Santa Ynez River near Live Oak picnic area.

*The Buckhorn Road just above its intersection with Camuesa Road.
Little Pine Mountain is in the distance.*

The first half mile is the toughest, a twisty, winding path leading up to the first of a number of saddles, short trials sections that provide a test of your riding ability. Undoubtedly you'll find yourself pushing a few of them. At the top the trail drops down into a brushy canyon and then up to a second saddle. Beyond this the countryside has been blackened by wildfire, and it has a different kind of beauty—that of nature's fire cycle—the chaparral undergoing the process of renewal.

Several gentle switchbacks take you down into a larger, more open canyon and the trail follows this downhill, then up and left over a third saddle. From here the route is almost continuous downhill, first across a large plateau, then through a small "window" between two knolls to a large flat bluff overlooking the river. Either the top of the knolls or the bluff provides a perfect lunch or picnic spot.

The trail drops off the west side of the bluff then continues across the river, where walking is mandatory over the large boulders. The swimming hole at Live Oak picnic area is .5 mile left. To complete the loop ride down Paradise Road 3 miles to Lower Oso, then 1.3 miles to your car at Upper Oso.

OLD MINE ROAD

TRAIL INFORMATION: Distance—7 miles Difficulty—Moderate
Topo—San Marcos Pass and Little Pine Mountain (Old Mine Road
not on the map)

RECREATIONAL MAP SERIES: Map No. 4—Santa Barbara
Mountain Bike Routes—Trail #12

HIGHLIGHTS: The Old Mine Road doesn't have a mine at its end,
just a series of tailings that remind you what it had once been used
for. But the short ride provides a pleasant way to explore the upper
end of Oso Canyon and to enjoy a small amount of single track
riding.

DIRECTIONS: From Upper Oso follow the road to Little Pine for 3.7
miles (.5 miles beyond Camuesa Connector) to a small saddle on the
left. Look for a dirt burm and fence.

CAUTION: The Buckhorn Road is open to ORV use. You should be
alert for their presence. Please be extremely cautious and on the
lookout for horse riders. The Santa Cruz Trail is used extensively
by them. Assume a rider is just around each corner. If necessary,
dismount from your bike and ask the horse rider what he/she would
like you to do.

Though the ride itself is short—only 7 miles—you can
combine the riding with creek exploration, lunch, or a picnic to
make it a longer, more enjoyable day's outing. The initial route
follows the Buckhorn Road for 3.5 miles. This section rises
relatively steeply to Camuesa Connector.

Along the way you'll have views of the front side of Little
Pine with you constantly, though the pedalling may be
strenuous enough to keep you from enjoying its beauty at this
point. But as your breath returns above Camuesa Connector

I'm sure you will enjoy it more and more. Beyond the Connector the main road continues to rise, though much more gradually. At first it curves around to the right around a ridgeline and then back to the left. As you get to the top of this ridge begin to look for a small road leading down and to the left at a diagonal. It shouldn't be too hard to spot.

The side road leads a mile downhill through serpentine outcroppings to a connector trail leading off to the left and down a steep hill (look carefully for it because the road continues on).

Before heading down the trail to Nineteen Oaks, you might continue along the connector road another .5 mile to the upper part of Oso Creek where a quicksilver (mercury) mine once existed. Beyond the tailings of the mine the creek is easy to follow, nice for an hour's exploration of the narrow chasm.

It is .4 miles on this to Nineteen Oaks Camp. Though short, be wary of this section because there are several steep parts with plenty of loose rock and serpentine to cause you problems. The steeper parts should be walked.

Just below Nineteen Oaks you will intersect the Santa Cruz Trail. From there it is 1.2 miles of wonderful single tracking to the Buckhorn Road and three-fourths miles on this to Upper Oso. While on the trail section below Nineteen Oaks RIDE EXTREMELY SLOWLY and keep a sharp lookout for hikers and horse riders. On the road be sure to look out for ORV riders.

BIG PINE ROAD
- → LITTLE PINE   3
- ← BLUFF CAMP   12
- → BIG PINE MOUNTAIN 17
- → HIDDEN POTRERO   4 →
LOS PADRES NATIONAL FOREST

BUCKHORN TRAIL

TRAIL INFORMATION: Distance—33 miles   Difficulty—
Strenuous to Hard Core   Topo—San Marcos Pass and Little Pine
Mountain

RECREATIONAL MAP SERIES: Map No. 4—Santa Barbara
Mountain Bike Routes—Trail #13

HIGHLIGHTS: This, the ride to Little Pine, and the Camuesa Loop
are the best three rides in the upper Santa Ynez River drainage.
This ride combines much of what the Little Pine Ride has to offer,
as well as 8 miles of exquisite single track riding in Buckhorn
Canyon and along lower Indian Creek. There is a real feeling of
wildness about the ride.

DIRECTIONS: From Upper Oso, ride up the road to Little Pine for
9.7 miles to the Buckhorn Trail intersection. The trail is 1.5 miles
beyond the switchbacks which lead across the steep east face of
Little Pine and has a trail sign marking it.

CAUTION: The Buckhorn Road is open to ORV use. You should be
alert for their presence. Please be extremely cautious and on the
lookout for horse riders. When you reach Indian Creek, the area
upstream is inside the Dick Smith Wilderness and is off-limits to
bikes. Please don't take your bike in the wilderness.

Either as a day trip or overnight, this trip allows the
possibility of exploring a relatively pristine and secluded part
of the back country. The first 7 miles of the route are along the
Buckhorn roadway, leading up past the Camuesa Road intersection (you'll come back out this way), up the Chalk Bluffs,
and up on the eastern shoulder of Little Pine Mountain.

A mile and a half after top top of the Bluffs, look for a trail
leading right and down into Buckhorn Canyon. An easily

spotted sign marks the trailhead. For 5 miles of very enjoyable riding, the trail leads down into Buckhorn Canyon,
through chaparral and winding canyon, thick with trees and
riparian growth and complete with a feeling of remoteness and
solitude.

At first the path drops steeply down through the chaparral.
The Monterey Shale is loose, making the riding somewhat
squirrely, and in places you will want to walk your bike. Then
it flattens out and enters a lovely, almost level canyon. Deep
and narrow, filled with a canopy of rose bushes, oak and
sycamore, you'll wish the trail would continue on forever and
ever. Unfortunately it lasts only 3 miles. You'll know you are
near the end when you reach Lower Buckhorn Camp, a half
mile up from Indian Creek. This would be a great place to stay
the night and an excellent base to use for exploring the Dick
Smith Wilderness by foot.

The good news is that this isn't the end of the single
tracking. There are still 4 miles of it ahead of you along Indian
Creek as it meanders down to Camuesa Road. At the lower
Indian Creek trailhead it is possible to turn left and follow
Pendola Road down Mono Creek and then to the Santa Ynez
River where you can follow the Gibraltar Trail back down
through Red Rock to Lower Oso and your car.

The best choice is to turn right and continue back up to
Buckhorn Road. It is 9.7 miles up to it and then 5 miles of
downhill back to Upper Oso.

For the first mile Camuesa Road rises steadily, then in the
next mile drops down into Camuesa Canyon. The downhill is
fun but unfortunately you lose everything you just gained. The
next 3 miles involves fairly easy but steady uphill riding
through oak meadows and short, narrow and pretty canyons.
Middle Camuesa Camp is 5.6 miles along the way. Beyond it
the road leads through a long, thin meadow for a mile then
turns left and ascends out of the canyon. In a mile you come to
a high point and from there you can see the Camuesa/Buckhorn
intersection.

A side road also leads from this point to the top of Camuesa Peak, which involves a gain of 300' and a mile's ride (have you got the energy?). From the top of the peak you'll find youself looking straight down on Gibraltar Reservoir. Look for the canyon on the north side of the lake which looks like it is filled with silt. Actually it is. This is where the material dredged from the lake's bottom (in a valiant effort to keep it from silting in) is being put.

From the high point, several short drops and climbs lead to Buckhorn Road and from there it is all downhill.

RED ROCK LOOP

TRAIL INFORMATION: Distance—6.5 miles   Difficulty—Moderately easy   Topo—Little Pine Mountain (river trail not shown on the map)

RECREATIONAL MAP SERIES: Map No. 4—Santa Barbara Mountain Bike Routes—Trail #14

HIGHLIGHTS: The Red Rock Trail allows you not only to an enjoyable 2-3 hour ride, but provides you with some of the best swimming holes on the river. This loop can be ridden from either direction. At the midpoint you'll find Gibraltar Dam and near the top of it a picnic area and a large board with interpretive information regarding the dam.

DIRECTIONS: From Lower Oso continue up the Santa Ynez River for 5 miles to a large open dirt parking area. From here you can ride either up the river or on a dirt road which proceeds uphill beyond a locked gate.

Though this area may have one of the largest concentrations of swimmers, sunbathers, picnickers, fishermen, and mountain bikers I fall in love with it every time I ride it, which is fairly often.

There are two choices—the low road or the high road. The low road goes up the river bed for a half mile to Red Rock, one of the most exquisite combinations of rock and emerald-green water anywhere.

But beware almost every year a careless swimmer is injured seriously here—mostly the dare devils who dive headfirst into the water. While it is deep in most places, in other places it is extremely shallow due to a number of large rocks hidden just underwater.

Gibraltar Dam, 3 miles upstream from Red Rock. It was constructed in the 1920s. More than 75% filled with silt, it is almost unusable.

Beyond Red Rock the road crosses the river and continues along a wide riverbed. Contorted layers of rock on the north side of the river show the extreme pressures which the shale must have undergone. Underfoot, if you look carefully, you can still find pieces of the red brick quicksilver kilns. Beyond this you'll find more pools as the road meanders back and forth across the river and through sycamore, cottonwood, and willow groves, meadows, and groves of live oak for several miles to Gibraltar Dam.

Depending on the time of year stream crossings may be wet or dry, and often spring floods litter the road with cobblestones, but despite this riding up the Santa Ynez River through this section is a pleasurable experience. Wear tennis shoes you don't mind getting wet and carry extra socks to put on afterwards and the ride will be even more enjoyable. Be cautious if the river is high. Stream crossings can be treacherous when you're trying to carry a bike on your shoulders.

The down side of riding the loop in this direction is that you've got a very steep half-mile climb to get up on the bench that takes you back to your car. The good news is that once you get up this hill the next 2.5 miles are almost all downhill. About a mile along the downhill section look for a trail which leads down through a saddle (the road turns to the right here). This is a little shorter and provides a last bit of single track.

If you decide to take the high road on the way in, look for a dirt road at the back side of the parking area. It is pretty obvious and beyond the locked gate climbs steadily (but not too steep) through a series of switchbacks for a mile up onto a wide open bench. The climb from here is gradual, leading to a high point from which you can see Gibraltar Dam. Then, hold onto your helmets the next half mile. You've got a big downhill ahead of you.

At the bottom, a short (but very steep) uphill leads to the top of the dam. The first pools are about a half mile downstream on the ride back down through the canyon.

GIBRALTAR TRAIL

TRAIL INFORMATION: Distance—Mine 6.5 miles; Forbush Trail 9 miles   Difficulty—Moderate to moderately strenuous   Topo—Little Pine Mountain (trail from Gibraltar Mine to Forbush Trail not on map)

RECREATIONAL MAP SERIES: Map No. 4—Santa Barbara Mountain Bike Routes—Trail #15

HIGHLIGHTS: When I feel like getting in a good ride—one with plenty of exercise and great scenery—this is the one I take. The ride provides views of Gibraltar Dam, a visit to a historic old quicksilver mine, and 3 miles of great single track riding on the Gibraltar Trail.

DIRECTIONS: From Red Rock, take either the high or low road to Gibraltar Dam. Continue up the road beyond the dam for a half mile to a closed gate (next to a large water tank). This road leads down to an inlet of the reservoir. Follow the right side of the inlet to the mouth of Gidney Creek, uphill, then east for 2.4 miles to the mine. Gibraltar Trail is just beyond this point.

CAUTION: The Sunbird Quicksilver Mine may contain harmful levels of mercury. While casual visits to look at the rusty old mine equipment may be safe, use extreme caution.

The portion of the Santa Ynez River beyond Gibraltar Dam is an area very few people know about. One of the reasons is that it is a long way there by foot. It offers interesting history at the Sunbird Quicksilver Mine and a section of trail that follows rolling hills of grass into the upper Santa Ynez area.

The feeling is one both of remoteness and rugged beauty, surprising in such close proximity to Santa Barbara's domestic water supply.

From the Red Rock parking area I usually take the high road, which is quicker, to Gibraltar Dam. Then I return on the low road for a quick dip.

Just beyond the dam the road up to Angostura Pass begins. Stay on this for a half mile until you come to a spur road next to a large water tank. The dirt road was built to service the quicksilver mines and until recently has been completely closed to vehicle traffic because of a slide across it.

This drops down to an inlet of Gibraltar Reservoir. If you feel frisky, look for a side trail leading left and out to the main body of water. It's technical and lots of fun. Beware, however, a tumble might take you into the reservoir.

The dirt road follows the right side of the inlet to Gidney Creek and then turns sharply left and up what seems like an interminable hill to a nice overlook of the reservoir. From here it is 2.4 miles of almost level riding to the Sunbird Mine.

While the mine is tempting to explore, a recent article about it in the Santa Barbara *News-Press* indicates that potentially dangerous levels of mercury may still be present.

Until recently the Forest Service was powerless to stop people from entering the old mine buildings while the claim was still active. However, the claim owner failed to re-file it in 1991, allowing control to revert to the federal government. Ultimately the Forest Service may end up razing the whole site, but until then more than likely you will see trail signs asking you not to enter the mine site.

Beyond the mine structures, the road continues a bit further. As you ride east it curves to the right around a hill for .2 mile. At this point it splits. The right fork takes you up a series of switchbacks which lead to other mine sites and rusting equipment. Eventually it deadends.

To continue upstream, take the left fork. The road winds to the right around another hill for a half mile and ends. The trail is on the left and cuts across a flat. Eventually it curves around a fairly large drainage and onto a high plateau covered with grassy slopes. You will gain several hundred feet on this uphill section and you may have to push some of it.

Above, on the plateau, the trail opens to intense views of the upper Santa Ynez. In the distance you can see the cottonwood-filled mouth of Mono Creek. The next several miles are some of the finest, almost level, though not quite, with the river beauty spread out below you, hanging just off the left side of your handlebars.

Return via the same route.

ANGOSTURA LOOP

TRAIL INFORMATION: Distance—14 miles   Difficulty—Moderately strenuous   Elevation Gain 2000'   Topo—San Marcos Pass and Little Pine Mountain

RECREATIONAL MAP SERIES: Map No. 4—Santa Barbara Mountain Bike Routes—Trail #6

HIGHLIGHTS: This route follows trails almost never used by horse riders or hikers, though you should always be on the lookout for them. It combines riding along the Santa Ynez River to Gibraltar Dam, a steady effort up the road to Angostura Pass, and a rewarding downhill on the Matias Potrero Trail back to the picnic area, where you can enjoy a lovely swim and a well-deserved B-B-Q.

DIRECTIONS: From Lower Oso continue up the Santa Ynez River for 2.5 miles to the Live Oak picnic area.

From the picnic area ride for several miles until you reach the Red Rock parking area. I usually take the high road to Gibraltar Dam because it is a little bit quicker. Just beyond the dam the road up to Angostura Pass begins.

Follow the road on past the turnoff to Gibraltar Mine. The first mile is steep. The climb is up and over a sandstone layer tilted on edge which lies on the north side of the Santa Ynez Fault. When you ride through a window cut in a thin layer of limestone (Sierra Blanca) the pedaling eases off. This is a good spot to take a break and enjoy the view west down the fault line, which is clearly visible.

Beyond, the circles around the upper end of Devil's Canyon, with small creeks filled with bay trees (and sometimes, even water) that provide a coolness and pleasant smell. Four miles from the dam Matias Potrero Trail drops down off the right side of the roadway. As it isn't marked with a sign you need to look for it carefully.

This trail drops down into Devil's Canyon and then eventually cuts across the north slope the mountains and along the Santa Ynez Fault for 6 miles. While it is possible to continue across the entire length of the Matias Potrero Trail to Arroyo Burro Road, two connector trails along the way lead down to the Santa Ynez River, each providing a better loop possibility. One in Devil's Canyon and the other near Live Oak Picnic Area (where you've parked).

The Devil's CanyonTrail intersects Matias Potrero about 1.5 miles down. This short route leads to the Santa Ynez River near the base of Gibraltar Dam. From there you can ride down the river past Red Rock and back to the picnic area. To do so, turn right at the Devil's Canyon intersection and continue 1.5 miles across the grassy slopes and through its picturesque narrows to the dam.

My preference is to continue on Matias Potrero Trail. It is a bit shorter, but more importantly, allows you continue the single track riding all the way back to your car. From Devil's Canyon, Matias Potrero continues for 2.5 miles along the fault and a number of grassy ridgelines to the spur leading down to Live Oak picnic area. You may notice a number of burned-out areas on the way. These are the result of prescribed burns conducted by the Forest Service.

The spur road is fairly obvious and from there it is a mile down to Paradise Road. Ride slowly. The dirt spur is rutted and loose rocks make it a bit tricky, especially the last 100 yards. Live Oak is 200 yards to the right on Paradise Road.

CAMUESA LOOP

TRAIL INFORMATION: Distance—33 miles Difficulty—Strenuous
Topo—San Marcos Pass and Little Pine Mountain

RECREATIONAL MAP SERIES: Map No. 4—Santa Barbara
Mountain Bike Routes—Trail #16

HIGHLIGHTS: This is a long loop that I probably do more than any
other. Linking the lower and upper Santa Ynez river canyons, and
skirting the edge of the Dick Smith Wilderness, the route passes
through almost every type of country that I like. Along the way you
can enjoy the historic Sunbird Quicksilver Mine, the quiet beauty
of the upper Santa Ynez River valley, excellent single track riding
on the Gibraltar and Mono trails, a dip (or incredibly exciting slide
down the face) in the pool at Mono Debris Dam, or a hot tub in the
relaxing waters of Little Caliente Hot Springs. Properly outfitted,
this makes for a nice overnight trip.

DIRECTIONS: Start at Lower Oso picnic area, which is 5 miles east
of Highway 154, and just across the first stream crossing in the
Santa Ynez River.

CAUTION: ORV enthusiasts use Camuesa and Buckhorn Roads.
Be on the lookout for these vehicles.

From Lower Oso, ride for 5 miles on pavement to the Red
Rock parking area and from there follow directions for the
Gibraltar Trail ride. Once on Gibraltar Trail, notice the thick
cottonwoods that you can see at the mouth of Mono Creek. This
is where you'll be heading. Near its intersection with the Cold
Springs trail, the trail is somewhat washed out so please take
care.

At the Cold Springs intersection head downstream (if you
go up trail you'll push almost all the way to the crest). It is just

When water is running down the face of Mono Debris Dam, you can climb up and slide down. The dam was built in the 1930s.

over a half mile of single tracking down to the Santa Ynez River. The route here isn't obvious. Turn left and go down river about 50 yards. You should see the trail leading across the river (actually just a small stream most of the time). You can probably ride across it, but if you prefer to make sure your shoes and socks stay dry, take them off first.

On the other side this incredibly beautiful path turns into the Mono Trail, which leads .through a half mile of riparian vegetation to Mono Creek. The 1.5 mile ride up it winds through the clusters of cottonwood seen from above, so thick that they form a tunnel of greenery. The trail ends at Mono Camp, an open area situated in a scattering of huge oak trees near the base of Mono Debris Dam.

The dam was built in the 1930s after a huge wildfire (232,000 acre Matilija Fire) burned from Ventura into many of the drainages upstream from Gibraltar Dam. Several debris dams were built to check the flow of sediment. Mono Debris Dam was silted in by 1938, just 2 years after its construction. Ironically, the rich silt left above and just below the Dam provided an excellent habitat for cottonwoods and willows, and the Least Bell's Vireo, a small bird now on the Endangered Species List. The bird has kept the city of Santa Barbara from raising the level of Gibraltar Dam.

This is a nice place for lunch. Walk your bikes the 50 yards to the water hole and stop for a dip. If water is running down the front of the dam, the truly hard core will also take time to climb the rope leading to the top and then slide back down into the pool. The drop is 80 feet and is steep as anything you'll find at Magic Mountain. One caution. Wear rugged shorts. The stretch fabric in bike pants wears out fast.

A short road leads out to Pendola Road. Turn left and ride along it through open meadows. In a half mile look for a road leading to the right. This leads up into the Mono Creek drainage. A mile up it you'll discover Little Caliente Hot Springs, which are actually not that hot, but thoroughly wonderful anyway, especially in the spring when the view out from this natural hot tub is of hills filled with wildflowers.

Return back to Pendola Road and continue up it. It crosses Mono Creek and then within a few yards begins to follow Indian Creek, crossing it several times. In a mile look for the Indian Creek trailhead on the right. I usually ride up the trail just a bit to a small check dam and replenish my water supply. I've used it a lot and never had problems, but to be cautious, I would recommend treatment before drinking it.

Just beyond the trailhead you'll find a locked gate across the road. This the start of Camuesa Road and the end of auto traffic, though it is open to ORV use and you should be on the lookout for them.

For the first mile Camuesa Road rises steadily, then in the next mile drops down into Camuesa Canyon. The downhill is fun but unfortunately you lose everything you just gained. The next 3 miles involves fairly easy but steady uphill riding through oak meadows and short, narrow and pretty canyons. Middle Camuesa Camp is 5.6 miles along the way. Beyond it the road leads through a long, thin meadow for a mile then turns left and ascends out of the canyon. In a mile you come to a high point and from there you can see the Camuesa/Buckhorn intersection.

A side road also leads from this point to the top of Camuesa Peak, which involves a gain of 300' and a mile's ride (have you got the energy?). From the top of the peak you'll find youself looking straight down on Gibraltar Reservoir. Look for the canyon on the north side of the lake which looks like it is filled with silt. Actually it is. This is where the material dredged from the lake's bottom (in a valiant effort to keep it from silting in) is being put.

From the high point, several short drops and climbs lead to Buckhorn Road and from there it is all downhill.

Upper Santa Ynez River Canyon

From the crest, just east of the top of Gibraltar Road, you can see out over the Santa Ynez River canyon. Looking almost directly below, you can see the upper end of Gibraltar Reservoir, its blue water looking like a jewel shimmering in the midst of an otherwise dull-green landscape.

Three major drainages feed into the lake—Indian and Mono creeks; the Agua Caliente drainage; and the upper Santa Ynez. Your gaze will naturally seem to follow the contours of the canyon upstream and into these watersheds. They feed from springs located high in the San Rafael Mountains: Indian Creek originates on Big Pine Mountain near Bluff Camp; Mono Creek on the upper edge of Madulce Peak.

Two miles from the upper end of the reservoir, Mono Creek enters It is easily spotted by the fan-shaped cluster of cottonwood trees and willows at its base. Following this drainage almost directly north leads your eye into wild country, the Dick Smith Wilderness. Just above Mono Debris Dam the creek splits into two forks, both of which eventually lead into it.

As your gaze wanders to the right, the second major drainage that comes into view is the Agua Caliente —where you'll find a relaxing hot springs (one of Knapp's country retreats was located here), Big Caliente Debris Dam, and in the upper canyon, exquisitely eroded sandstone.

If you need help or information, Pendola Ranger Station is located at the base of Agua Caliente Canyon, which can be located by two major peaks to be found directly behind it—the

Hildreth peaks. Both are over 5000' in elevation. Beyond them
is the upper end of Mono Creek

To the far right is the upper Santa Ynez river drainage. If
you look closely you can spot Jameson Reservoir (Juncal Dam),
a small body of water owned by the Montecito Water District.
Beyond the lake, a wall of mountains define the boundary
between Santa Barbara and Ventura counties. In air miles
from Jameson Reservoir, the rural community of Ojai is
actually not too far. The wall is formed by two massive
mountains, Old Man Mountain and Monte Arido. Old Man has
sort of a pointed look to it, with the points leaning somewhat
to the right.

In these canyons you will find some of the finest mountain
bike riding that Santa Barbara has to offer.

Camping

There are four car campgrounds located in the upper Santa
Ynez River canyon. Juncal Camp is located in the Santa Ynez
River drainage and is the first you will come to. Mid-Santa
Ynez and P-Bar Flats are located in the open bottom lands of
the Agua Caliente watershed, not too far from the Pendola
Ranger Station. Mono Camp is the furthest, and is just below
the confluence of Indian and Mono Creeks.

While there are no fees for using these campsites, no water
is available at them, so you'll need to bring an adequate supply
with you. Camping is on a first come, first serve basis and the
limit you may stay is 14 days.

Primitive area camping is also available, either by backpack
or mountain bike. Blue Canyon, the upper Santa Ynez River,
Mono Creek, and Indian Creek all have sites which may be
used. Camping is in established campsites only and fires must
be kept to the facilities provided by the Forest Service. This is
a one-way in, one-way out canyon and if a wildfire should
occur, it is a long way out.

Overnight camping is not permitted at either of the hot
springs.

Picnicking

There's usually a table available at any of the camps with the exception of holiday weekends such as Lincoln or Washington's birthdays or the Memorial Day and July 4th periods. Plus there are plenty of places to hunker down for a feast right by the river.

You will also find two established picnic areas in Agua Caliente Canyon—Lower Caliente and Big Caliente, which is located at the hot springs.

Mileage Log From the Top of Gibraltar Road

0.0   Intersection of Camino Cielo and Gibraltar roads

3.0   Cold Springs/Forbush Flats trailheads

3.2   San Ysidro trailhead

5.8   Romero Saddle

7.0   Start of the Divide Peak ORV trailhead

7.6   Escondido Creek

9.0   Blue Canyon trailhead

10.4 Juncal Camp

13.4 Agua Caliente Canyon/Pendola Ranger Station

13.5 Mid-Santa Ynez Camp

14.1 P-Bar Flats Camp

14.7 Access road to Santa Ynez River

17.0 Mono Camp/Debris Dam

18.0 Mono Creek Road/Little Caliente Hot Springs

19.2 Indian Creek trailhead

19.3 Locked Gate/Beginning of the Camuesa Road

MURIETTA DIVIDE

TRAIL INFORMATION: Distance—3 miles from Juncal Camp to Jameson Reservoir; 6 miles to Murietta Divide   Elevation Gain—450' to reservoir; 1600' to the Divide   Difficulty—Easy to reservoir, moderate to Murietta Divide   Topo—Carpinteria and White Ledge Peak

RECREATIONAL MAP SERIES: Map No. 4—Santa Barbara Mountain Bike Routes—Trail #19

HIGHLIGHTS: The route to Jameson reservoir and beyond to the Divide provides a leisurely ride up into the upper end of the Santa Ynez drainage. The reservoir is picturesque and on the north side large slabs of sandstone provide a scenic backdrop. Alder Creek is located in a small but very pretty canyon that is filled with its namesake—alder trees. A short spur leads to the mouth of this enchanting place.

DIRECTIONS: Follow Gibraltar Road for 7 miles to Camino Cielo. Turn right. Follow the crest road for 5.8 miles to Romero Saddle then drop down an additional 4.6 miles on the rough dirt road until you reach Juncal Camp, which is located just across the Santa Ynez River. The road leading to Jameson Reservoir is directly behind (east of) the camp.

The lower part of the ride begins at the back of Juncal Camp at a locked gate and follows a graded dirt road up the left side of the valley for 2.5 miles to the reservoir. This section has scattering of oak trees, meadows, and if the reservoir is spilling, a crystal clear creek. Near the base of the reservoir you'll encounter the only major climb, a 300' elevation gain which brings you out on the right side of the lake, which is owned by the Montecito Water District.

From this point the road continues along the water's edge, eventually leading to the upper end of the watershed at a saddle known as Murietta Divide. About a half mile from the dam look for a side road leading to the right and down. This is the turnoff to Alder Creek. You'll know you're near when you see the water flume leading from the creek.

A quarter mile of pedaling across a meadow leads you to the mouth of the canyon and the beginning of a beautiful hike along pools and waterfalls and an abundance of creekside vegetation.

The reservoir road continues to the east, dropping down a bit, then climbing back up near the end of the lake. The area above the reservoir is known as Billiard Flats and is composed of open meadows and rolling hills. Due to the Ojai Fire of 1985, which burned this area, the Flats is still open enough for you to walk off-trail if you want to take a break. Beyond Billiard Flats the canyon again narrows and begins to climb to Murietta Divide which is 2 miles above the upper end of the reservoir.

You will find year round water at a small camp (Santa Ynez) just before you reach the Divide.

If you've made arrangements with very, very good friends to pick you up in Ojai at the day's end, you can actually continue east and down into the Matilija drainage, which eventually leads to Highway 33 about 5 miles above Ojai. Down canyon you will find a second overnight camp— Murietta—and below that a private hot springs and near the highway, Matilija Reservoir.

My dream trip is being dropped off at the top of Gibraltar Road, then pedaling across the east end of Camino Cielo, down Pendola Road to Juncal, and from there riding up over Murietta Divide and down into Ojai.

PENDOLA LOOP

TRAIL INFORMATION: Distance—6 miles to Murietta Divide; 25 miles for loop Elevation Gain—1600' to Murietta Divide; 4000' to Monte Arido Difficulty—Moderate to Hard Core Topo—Carpinteria, White Ledge Peak, Old Man Mountain and Hildreth Peak

RECREATIONAL MAP SERIES: Map No. 4—Santa Barbara Mountain Bike Routes—Trail #19

HIGHLIGHTS: The view from the top of Monte Arido is one of the best. Not only do you have the entire Santa Barbara backcountry at your fingertips, but all of Ventura County as well. The 6 miles from Murietta Divide to the top of 6003' Monte Arido is tough, but the reward is well worth it—10 miles of pure excitement.

DIRECTIONS: Same as for Murietta Divide

CAUTION: This is an extremely long trip and should be done only if you are in great shape. The top of Monte Arido is not the place to have problems. Be sure you are fully prepared.

This is the ultimate day's loop trip. The route follows the upper Santa Ynez River for 6 miles from Juncal Camp past Jameson Reservoir to Murietta Divide. This is the easy part of the trip. At the Divide you turn left (north) and from there the road leads sharply uphill across the flanks of Old Man Mountain to Monte Arido. You'll push a lot of this if you aren't in top shape because it is very steep and loose in places. Once beyond Old Man Mountain the gradient does ease off, though by this time you will have pretty tired legs.

Santa Ynez Camp, .5 miles below Murietta Divide, provides the last source of water as well as a very pleasant overnight camp. Be sure to carry plenty for the ride beyond the camp.

Though difficult, the 6 mile "section from hell" from Murietta Divide to the top of Monte Arido provides spectacular scenery, including island views, the southern Sierras, and most of the Santa Barbara and Ventura back countries. The last time I rode this there was snow on top of the high peaks and bear prints (both mother and cub) that had to have been made that day, because the snow had fallen just the night before.

The Pendola Jeep Trail is half mile beyond (north of) the top of Monte Arido and is easy to spot. It leads left down into a canyon, then eventually along a long ridgeline which winds up and down for 10 miles to Pendola Ranger Station. From there, turn left on Pendola Road. It is 3 miles back to Juncal Camp and your car.

A last note—use good sense on the way up. If you don't think you can make it all the way, turn back. It's all downhill the way you came and even from the top of Monte Arido it shouldn't take you more than an hour to get back to your car. Once on the Pendola Jeepway, however, you are committed.

AGUA CALIENTE

TRAIL INFORMATION: Distance— 3 miles to Hot Springs; 8 miles to the end of the upper canyon   Elevation Gain—200' to hot springs; 800' to end of upper canyon   Difficulty—Easy to Moderate
TOPO: Hildreth Peak (the connector from Agua Caliente Canyon to the Hildreth Jeep Trail is not on the map)

RECREATIONAL MAP SERIES: Map No. 4—Santa Barbara Mountain Bike Routes—Trail #18

HIGHLIGHTS: The upper part of the Agua Caliente drainage contains a very relaxing hot springs, beautiful sandstone formations, and a huge debris dam. Beyond the dam the country has a wild and romantic feel to it. This is one of my favorite places.

DIRECTIONS: Follow Gibraltar Road for 7 miles to Camino Cielo. Turn right. Follow the crest road for 5.8 miles to Romero Saddle then drop down an additional 4.6 miles on the rough dirt road until you reach Juncal Camp. Continue past the camp an additional 3 miles until you reach the intersection of the road leading to the Pendola Hot Springs. Park near the intersection.

Agua Caliente is the name of this canyon—the place of the warm water. For me the water temperature is about perfect—105 degrees at the hottest. But while many people know about the Big Caliente Hot Springs, very few know that one of Santa Barbara's nicest canyons is to be found above them.

The canyon is composed of two major drainages—Devil's Canyon and Agua Caliente proper. Both have exquisite sandstone formations in them, with narrow, steep-walled sections that are almost like works of art. To reach these you will need to do some scrambling.

The first 3 miles of the ride from the Ranger Station is on a dirt road which is almost level and follows Agua Caliente

Creek. The river bottom is fairly open at first but after the first mile the canyon narrows. Several river crossings bring you to the hot springs. There is a changing area there (if you've brought a swim suit) and the tub itself is a square cement pool about 10' x 10'.

Beyond the parking area the dirt road turns into a trail. This marks the beginning of the upper canyon. As you start up the trail, look across the creek and about 150' up the side of the mountain. This is actually where the hot springs are located. The water is piped down to the cement pool where people bathe. A friendly reminder in the winter—when you use the hot springs, don't turn the water from the springs off completely. Allowing even a little of the water to flow through the pipes keeps it from freezing and damaging the pipes.

The single track from the hot springs leads along the left side of the canyon for a half mile then crosses the creek and climbs up the right side of Big Caliente Debris Dam, built to help keep sediment from spilling down into Gibraltar Reservoir. The grade is fairly gentle and easy to ride and there is a great swimming hole at the base of the dam.

Beyond the dam is a mile of wonderful riding through a forest of cottonwoods (*los alamos* in Spanish). Just beyond this you'll cross to the left side of Agua Caliente Creek. In a hundred yards, Devil's Canyon comes in from the right. I like hiking up into this drainage though you will have to scramble up the creek to do so.

The main trail continues up Agua Caliente Canyon, which turns sharply to the left. The canyon is relatively narrow and has a wilderness quality to it that I appreciate. The narrows are interspersed with open, grassy meadows which make this an extremely beautiful canyon. A mile up you'll find a small overnight spot, Agua Caliente Camp, which provides a great base from which to explore the upper canyon. Two more miles of relatively level riding (or hiking) brings you to the upper canyon and a series of exquisite sandstone formations. One note—you will have to walk your bike through a number of stream crossings. But when you get back to your car at the end of your ride, a great hot tub awaits you.

MONO TRAIL

TRAIL INFORMATION: Distance—Variable Elevation Loss—
Relatively level Difficulty—Easy Topo—Little Pine Mountain
and Hildreth Peak

HIGHLIGHTS: Mono Trail is part of the historic route from Santa
Barbara to the Cuyama Valley. The section from Mono Camp to the
river is 1.5 miles in length and is one of the most scenic rides in the
backcountry. The lower canyon is filled with cottonwood trees and
they form a canopy for your hike to the river. You can continue
another mile upstream, cross the river, and work your way along
the right bank to gain access either to Blue Canyon or Agua Caliente
Canyon.

DIRECTIONS: Follow Gibraltar Road for 7 miles to Camino Cielo.
Turn right. Follow the crest road for 5.8 miles to Romero Saddle
then drop down an additional 4.6 miles on the rough dirt road until
you reach Juncal Camp. Continue past the camp an additional 6
miles until you reach Mono Camp. The trail begins at the lower end
of the camp.

This is a trail that I wish would go on forever and forever.
The canyon through which it passes is filled with cottonwood
trees and thick stands of willows, the canopy completely
covering the trail and providing the feeling that you are
walking through a tunnel of greenery. It is the home of a tiny
bird known as the Least Bell's Vireo, a migratory bird that is
on the Endangered Species List. There are roughly only 300
known pairs of them left and approximately 50-60 of these
pairs make this area their spring and summer home.

Mono Trail begins at the lower end of Mono Camp. Though
it isn't that easy to spot, you shouldn't have too much trouble
locating it. Look for a path that takes off through the brush. A

hundred yards after you pass through a long grass meadow the canopy closes in overhead, and from here on the trail curves back and forth through the cottonwood forest for a half mile, finally straightening out somewhat for the last mile which is along the left side of the canyon.

Near the mouth of the canyon the trail rises slightly and then turns sharply left and into the Santa Ynez River drainage. Mono Trail continues for a mile along the left side of the river and ends near the bottom of the Cold Springs Trail. From here a number of possibilities await you. A half mile up Cold Springs Trail (mostly pushing) you'll intersect Gibraltar Trail which you can take to the Sunbird Quicksilver Mine.

If you work your way along the right side of the river through a series of willow thickets you come out on a dirt road that will take you to the lower end of Blue Canyon which you can ride up, or you can turn left near the mouth and recross the river and continue on the dirt road over to the P-Bar Flats area. A short distance to the right leads to the Pendola Ranger Station and Agua Caliente Canyon. A turn to the left takes you up and over a ridge and back to Mono Debris Dam.

At the crest of the ridge, look for a trail leading left. This leads back down to the Mono Trail and allows you to avoid a portion of the main road.

MONO CANYON

TRAIL INFORMATION: Distance—1 mile to hot springs; 5 miles
to Ogilvy Ranch; 10 miles to Mono Narrows Elevation Gain—300'
to ranch; 700' to Narrows   Difficulty—Moderate to strenuous
Topo—Hildreth Peak

RECREATIONAL MAP SERIES: Map No. 4—Santa Barbara
Mountain Bike Routes—Trail #17

HIGHLIGHTS: Upper Mono Canyon has a dirt road for 5 miles to
the historic Ogilvy Ranch and from there a trail for the next 5 miles
to the Mono Narrows. The Narrows contain one of Santa Barbara's
largest and most beautiful set of pools. At the end of the ride a
refreshing dip in Little Caliente Hot Springs awaits you. The ranch
itself is still private and is off limits.

DIRECTIONS: Follow Gibraltar Road for 7 miles to Camino Cielo.
Turn right. Follow the crest road for 5.8 miles to Romero Saddle
then drop down an additional 4.6 miles on the rough dirt road until
you reach Juncal Camp. Continue past the camp an additional 7
miles (1 mile beyond Mono Camp) until you reach the intersection
leading to Mono Creek. Either park here or turn right and drive up
this road 1 mile to a locked gate near Little Caliente Hot Springs.

Though privately owned and off limits, the Ogilvy Ranch is
symbolic of Santa Barbara's pioneer heritage. The first in-
habitant to settle in Mono Canyon was Joe Hildreth who
built a one-room cabin and named his 160-acre homestead *San
Garbacia*. Eventually he gave half his land to a friend named
Carl Stoddard, the only proviso being that he also build a cabin
on his portion.

Both men were later hired by the Forest Service in the early
1900s after this area was included in the Forest Reserve
system. Later, the entire holdings was sold to Arthur Ogilvy

and though it has been resold several times since, the ranch
has still retained Ogilvy's name.

The first mile of the ride from the intersection of the
Pendola and Mono roads is actually up the Little Caliente
drainage. The grade is not too steep until near the end when
the road rises up over a saddle and drops into the Mono
watershed. Near the top of this rise a small turnout and
parking area marks the start of a short walk to the Little
Caliente Hot Springs. These are set in the side of the hill and
are a more natural version of the hot springs in Aqua Caliente
Canyon.

A locked gate across the road bars further vehicle travel.
From here it is 5 miles to the Ogilvy Ranch. The creek runs
most of the winter and through early summer and the road
crosses it a number of times. Some of the crossings can be a bit
deep and you might want to check a few of them out before
crashing on through. Wearing a pair of tennis shoes you don't
mind getting wet isn't a bad idea either.

As you near the ranch, look for a trail that stays on the right
side of the creek. This is the way around the ranch. It leads up
on a bluff from which you have excellent views of it. The next
5 miles of riding are strictly on trail. The path crosses the creek
a number of times, and though most of this isn't technical
riding, you'll probably have to walk most of the crossings and
some of the trail sections.

Near the end of the 10 mile ride the canyon gets quite
narrow and there is some technical riding just before you get
to the Narrows. The trail crosses a small side creek and just
past this it turns left and begins to head directly up a
steep hill. The Mono Narrows is just beyond this. To reach
them you will have to scramble for about a half mile up the
creek to the pools. The first several are plenty deep and far
nicer than most you find in the backcountry, but they are only
a glimmer of what lies ahead.

Just above are two huge water holes. The first is 30 feet
wide and at least 60 feet long. The only way to continue
upstream is to swim. The biggest pool lies just a bit further and

makes the swim worth it. It is 40 feet wide and more than 100'
long. There are plenty of places to kick back and enjoy the sun,
and if you continue on past the last pool, the upper part of
Mono Creek is pleasant to explore. Alamar Creek enters
on the left, a half mile above the Narrows.

On the way back, stop at the hot springs for a dip. The water
isn't as hot as you might want it to be, but it feels great.

INDIAN CREEK

TRAIL INFORMATION: Distance—4 miles to Lower Buckhorn
Elevation Gain—350' Difficulty—Moderate Topo—Indian Creek

RECREATIONAL MAP SERIES: Map No. 4—Santa Barbara
Mountain Bike Routes—Trail #13

HIGHLIGHTS: The lower Indian drainage is almost level and
winds through scenic sandstone and shale formations and very
pretty riparian vegetation. There are numerous pools and the
fishing is rumored to be great. Lower Buckhorn Camp is 4 miles
from the trailhead.

DIRECTIONS: Follow Gibraltar Road for 7 miles to Camino Cielo.
Turn right. Follow the crest road for 5.8 miles to Romero Saddle
then drop down an additional 4.6 miles on the rough dirt road until
you reach Juncal Camp. It is an additional 8.2 miles on Pendola
Road to the Indian Creek trailhead (2.2 beyond Mono Camp and 100
yards before a locked gate across the road).

CAUTION: The area beyond Buckhorn Creek is inside the Dick
Smith Wilderness and is closed to mountain bikes. Please respect
this.

Just the name—Indian Creek—has a wonderful sound.
The creek is worthy of a name in itself. It is almost level, and
thus makes for an easy ride, with lots of meanders that create
small little meadows and elbows that hide deep pools. It is a
lovely place to go. The riding, however, is somewhat technical
and you will have to carry your bike across almost every creek
crossing.

The trailhead tells little of what lies ahead. It is just a small,
open parking lot on the edge of the chaparral. The first quarter

mile is up the left side of the creek to a small debris dam (a great pool for the end of the hike). Most of the time you'll have to wade through the pool. In fifty yards you cross back again though here the crossing isn't very deep. Your best bet is to wear tennis shoes that you don't mind getting wet.

You'll notice that you are still on a jeep road at this point. Follow this for .3 miles up over one short but very steep hill (you'll walk this one) and then another .5 miles. The road turns sharply to the left at the end of a long ridge (the creek makes a u-shaped bend around this ridge) and then crosses to the right side of the creek.

At the point where the jeep road crosses to the right side of the creek, look for the trail. It is on the left and follows the creek. The jeep road veers to the right and begins to climb steeply up the mountainside. Do not take this route unless you love to punish yourself.

Beyond this you will have no trouble following the trail along Indian Creek. It is a wonderful ride and worthy of a full day. Lower Buckhorn Camp is 4 miles. The trail up this side canyon provides a very picturesque way to extend your ride a bit. It leads up onto the eastern side of Little Pine Mountain. The trail is fairly level and winds back and forth across the small creek and through a lovely canyon. Deep and narrow, it is filled with a canopy of rose bushes, oak and sycamore. You'll wish the trail would continue on forever and ever. Unfortunately it lasts only 3 miles.

Beyond this the trail is too steep and loose to ride and no fun at all to push.

CAMUESA PEAK

TRAIL INFORMATION: Distance—11 miles   Elevation Gain—
1600'   Difficulty—Moderately strenuous   Topo—Little Pine

RECREATIONAL MAP SERIES: Map No. 4—Santa Barbara
Mountain Bike Routes—Trail #16

HIGHLIGHT: Camuesa Canyon is a long, narrow valley that
alternates between short steep climbs through narrow canyons and
open oak covered meadows. The place has a wild, remote feeling to
it. Near the upper end you can ride out to Camuesa Peak, which
looks straight down on Gibraltar Reservoir and the quicksilver
mines.

CAUTION: The Camuesa Road is open to ORV use. You should be
alert for their presence. Please be extremely cautious and on the
lookout for them.

For the first mile Camuesa Road rises steadily up through
a narrow drainage, then in the next mile drops down into
Camuesa Canyon. The downhill is fun but unfortunately you
lose everything you just gained. The next 3 miles involves
fairly easy but steady uphill riding through oak meadows and
short, narrow and pretty canyons. Middle Camuesa Camp is
5.6 miles along the way. Beyond it the road leads through a
long, thin meadow for a mile then turns left and ascends out
of the canyon. In a mile you come to a high point and from there
you can see the Camuesa/Buckhorn intersection.

A side road also leads from this point to the top of Camuesa
Peak, which involves a gain of 300' and a 2 mile ride (have you
got the energy?). From the top of the peak you'll find yourself
looking straight down on Gibraltar Reservoir. Look for the

canyon on the north side of the lake which looks like it is filled
with silt. Actually it is. This is where the material dredged
from the lake's bottom (in a valiant effort to keep it from silting
in) is being put.

HILDRETH OVERNIGHT

TRAIL INFORMATION: Distance—Hildreth Overnight 42 miles;
Pendola Overnight 46 miles Difficulty—Strenuous Topo—Rancho
Nuevo Creek, Old Man Mountain and Hildreth Peak

RECREATIONAL MAP SERIES: Map No. 4—Santa Barbara
Mountain Bike Routes—Trail #20

HIGHLIGHTS: This overnight trip provides a way to experience a
combination of the Ventura and Santa Barbara backcountry areas.
The route crosses the highest part of the eastern end of the Santa
Ynez River drainage and provides exciting downhill and spectacular scenery.

DIRECTIONS: From Santa Barbara, drive down Highway 101 to
Ventura, then follow Highway 33 for 11 miles to Ojai. Continue
another 30 miles on Highway 33 to a point just before Pine
Mountain Summit where a dirt road with a locked gate leads to the
west (left). The route begins here. This portion of it is well illustrated
on Recreational Map #3, Dick Smith Wilderness.

While there are many overnight bike camping trips you
can make by combining sections of previously mentioned
roads and trails, several other long trips can be made across
the heart of the backcountry and back to Santa Barbara, trips
perfect for a Friday afternoon to Sunday period of time. These
rides do, however, require you to have a friend drive you to the
starting point.

The first night's stop can be made 5 miles up the dirt road
at Potrero Seco, a grassy oak-shaded camp. While there is a
nearby stream, it is intermittent. La Jolla Spring, some
distance down the creekbed, runs year round. Or if you wish,
start early on Saturday morning and ride on through Potrero

Seco and continue on down to P-Bar Flats for the night. If you do the ride on a moonlit weekend, you can ride up to the Big Caliente Hot Springs by its silvery light and sooth those aching muscles.

A mile and a half beyond Potrero Seco you'll come to a junction. The right road heads to Don Victor Valley. A 26 mile ride along the edge of the Dick Smith Wilderness is possible by following this road, but there are some seriously steep uphill and downhill sections along it and unless you love pushing your bike (with overnight equipment this isn't easy) I wouldn't recommend it.

The main route leads predominantly south towards Monte Arido. You will reach a second junction 3 miles later. At this point you can turn right and ride across Hildreth Mountain into the upper Santa Ynez Valley. This jeepway ends near P-Bar Flats Campground, which is a great place to stay the second night. You can also continue on the main ridgeline to the Pendola Jeepway, which is 7 miles further.

The Hildreth Jeep Trail is 15 miles long and is composed of a series of ups and downs across Hildreth (5210') and Hildreth Peak (5065') and a long stretch of adrenalin-pumping downhill to P-Bar Flats. Both jeepways end conveniently near the Big Caliente Hot Springs.

On the last day you can either ride up Pendola Road to Romero Saddle and ride down this to town or continue across Camino Cielo and go down this. To make your last day as much a backcountry experience as possible, you might consider riding up Camuesa Road and going down to Upper Oso instead.

 # Figueroa Mountain

As you crest San Marcos Pass, Figueroa is the first part of the San Rafael range that comes into view. It is roughly 25 air miles from Santa Barbara, far enough to the interior to escape much of the coastal haze that sometimes restricts views from the Santa Ynez Mountains and high enough in elevation to provide a change in the seasons.

The road distance is approximately 45 miles—just over an hour's drive—from the intersection of Highways 101 and 154 to Figueroa's 4,528 foot crest. Psychologically, this may be one of the shortest drives you can take to get the furthest away from what is typically Santa Barbara: chaparral-covered hills that never seem to change and seasons that always seem the same.

View From the Top

From the Lookout Tower located on top of the mountain, 360 degree views of much of the County greet you. To the south are the Santa Ynez Mountains, from this perspective truly a mountain wall. On a clear day the Channel Islands shimmer on the horizon, so close that you can almost reach out and touch them.

As you drop your gaze to the foreground you look out over the Santa Ynez Valley, its open expanses of grassland dotted with Valley Oaks, a land that turns green in January while the high country is filling with snow. Above and to the west is Point Conception, a land revered by the Chumash, the place of the setting sun, where these Indians believed they would travel in the life that comes after death.

View from the Zaca Peak Overlook towards Figueroa Mountain.

Turning north, to the right, the rugged San Rafael Wilderness comes into view, where exploration of this pristine country is by foot travel only. If you know just where to look you can spy Pool Rock and Condor Cave, formations that may have marked an important winter solstice site for the Chumash. In the distance, looming over the thin knife blade edge of Hurricane Deck, are the Sierra Madre Mountains, a relatively even-crested range that has magnificent potreros , or meadows, and ancient Chumash rock art sites.

Turning even further to the right, on the eastern horizon, 6593 foot San Rafael Mountain rises somewhat inauspiciously to a rounded summit. Hidden on its flanks, however, are the beautiful Mission pines, thought to have supplied the huge beams from which Franciscan fathers constructed the Santa Barbara Mission and magnificent sandstone outcroppings. Until they were taken into captivity, this is a place that I could count on seeing the endangered California condor soar across the sky. Perhaps on another day, if the Condor Recovery Program is successful, I will see them again.

Overnight Camping

Picnic areas, overnight camps, and numerous hiking trails provide excellent opportunities for solitary or family recreation. Choices range from exploration of historic mines or pioneer homesteads, a fishing expedition on Manzana Creek, a quiet lunch at Pino Alto or Cumbre picnic areas, or a more rustic feast under the forest canopy of East Pinery, a weekend camp out, nature study, or perhaps simply an afternoon drive to view the exquisite scenery. There are enough choices that you may want to spend a few days camping out in the Figueroa Mountain area.

There are four car campgrounds for those who wish to spend the night, all on a first come, first served basis: Figueroa and Cachuma Camp on the upper slopes of the mountain; Davy Brown and Nira on the lower north side near the edge of the San Rafael Wilderness. Figueroa and Davy Brown camps both usually have running water, as well as a $5 overnight fee.

Recently, however, due to an extended drought, neither camp has had water available. Check with the Forest Service about the current situation before heading up here.

Though Cachuma Camp and Nira do not have an overnight fee, neither camp facility has running water.

The Mountain Biking

Figueroa Mountain offers incredibly wonderful—though often demanding—mountain biking opportunities. There is no more scenic or awe-inspiring landscape in Santa Barbara County than this mountainous country. I especially favor it in the summertime. Rarely does the temperature rise above the mid-80s and usually there is a cool breeze to soften the heat. Figueroa is perfect for late afternoons, since most of the trails lead down the shaded back side of the mountain and roads can be ridden back uphill just before sunset when it is cooler.

Most of the rides included are loops (which are my preference), with trails providing downhill sections and either dirt or paved roads the uphill portions. Be sure to carry plenty of water, a pump, tools, spare tube, and be ready to enjoy fantastic riding.

Topos

Two topographical maps, Figueroa Mountain and Bald Mountain, cover most of the routes included on this map. For routes to Zaca Peak and the area west of it you will also need the Zaca Lake topo. If you ride beyond Hell's Half Acre, the San Rafael Mountain topo might also be helpful.

PLEASE NOTE

RIDING MOUNTAIN BIKES IN THE SAN RAFAEL OR DICK SMITH WILDERNESSES IS EXPRESSLY FORBIDDEN. ENJOY THE BEAUTIFUL TRAIL COMPLEX OFFERED BY FIGUEROA MOUNTAIN AND PLEASE KEEP YOUR BIKE OUT OF THEM.

Figueroa Mountain Road

The view over the Santa Ynez Valley from the top of Fir Canyon is well worth the drive here, as is the mountain bike riding.

Fir Canyon

Just across the road from the trail leading down Fir Canyon to Davy Brown Campground, a large green outcropping of serpentine is exposed, its shiny, pointed surface marking what is the start of what I consider to be the prettiest canyon anywhere in Santa Barbara County.

The trail was built by Edgar Davidson, one of the first rangers to be stationed in this area when the Pine Mountain and Zaca Lake Forest Reserve was created in 1898. A bronze memorial plaque encased in serpentine that commemorates his efforts is located down the trail near the intersection with the Munch Canyon Connector.

Davidson's cabin was located a short distance down into Fir Canyon and from it he made regular patrols, watching out especially for careless campers who might start a forest fire, checking on grazing permits, and hacking out the trail systems we use today. His district included all of Figueroa Mountain and extended throughout most of what today is the San Rafael Wilderness.

Unfortunately, nothing remains of his cabin, though halfway down the trail you can still spot the remains of a cabin built by Harry Roberts in the 1920s to service chrome mining claims he had established on the east side of Figueroa Mountain. This old cabin was used as an overnight spot until several years ago when the roof collapsed. Today all that is left are the rotting remains of the log siding.

The canyon is narrow, alternating between long level sections which pass through thin-bedded layers of shale and steep plunges over boulder fields which form beautiful moss-covered waterfalls. Tall forests of big cone spruce grace the upper canyon, with bigleaf maple and oaks inhabiting the canyon bottoms.

The combination of cascading stream, deep pools, moss-covered rocks, and sense of pervading solitude provide a feeling that I never tire of. In the winter Fir Canyon takes on a different kind of color—hundreds of thousands of ladybugs migrate to the canyon from the Sierras. Thick blankets of the small insects cover downed logs, boulders, leaves, and tree branches and many other surfaces.

The trail drops down into Fir Canyon quickly, then meanders through a vee formed by Monterey shales gradually dropping downhill for a half-mile to a creek crossing. In another hundred yards a major side drainage comes in from the right. The main trail turns left, crosses the creek, and goes up and over a slight hill, then drops back down to the creek where you'll find the sign in memory of Edgar Davidson.

Look across the creek and you should spot a trail heading uphill that connects with Munch Canyon. As you continue down Fir Canyon, just a few yards below the Davidson sign look for the spur leading to Black Willow Springs Trail. It cuts diagonally up and to the left . This eventually leads to the Catway Road. Shortly below this is the ruins of Harry Roberts' cabin. An old road to the mining claims leads off to the right and up onto the northeastern side of Figueroa Mountain.

These connector trails form a network which make a variety of loop rides possible. The more you get to know the mountain, the larger the number of possibilities. Following the Munch spur leads for .6 mile to an intersection. Continuing straight ahead leads down into Munch Canyon and eventually Sunset Valley, while turning right will take you up a pleasant trail for a mile to the East Pinery loop.

From the Roberts' cabin, the Fir Canyon trail drops steeply, losing several hundred feet over the next half mile. There are numerous cascades and plenty of pools throughout. Below this the creek becomes level and quiet, the pools reflecting an image of serenity. Near the trail's end the canyon opens to a wide meadow, the former site of Davy Brown's cabin, and just beyond this it turns to the right, leading through a gate to the campground.

DIRECTIONS: Though the Davy Brown trailhead can be accessed from either end of the Figueroa Mountain Loop, the shortest route there is from the Los Olivos end of it. When you reach Los Olivos, turn north on Figueroa Mountain Road (next to Mattei's tavern). It is 14.5 miles to the trailhead, which is a half mile east of Figueroa Campground. There is a metal sign marking it and it is next to a prominent serpentine outcropping that is difficult to miss. The trail leads to the left, over an open grassy hill and down into Fir Canyon.

TOPOS—Two topographical maps—Figueroa Mountain and Bald Mountain—cover most of the area included in the rides.

FIR CANYON/JEEPWAY

TRAIL INFORMATION: Distance —11.4 miles   Elevation Loss—
1750' down to Davy Brown; 1900' elevation gain back up to Catway
Difficulty—Strenuous with some technical riding

SANTA BARBARA RECREATIONAL MAP SERIES: Map #5—
Figueroa Mountain Hiking and Biking Routes—Trail #2

HIGHLIGHTS: This is the prettiest canyon in Santa Barbara. From
its pine crested start atop Figueroa Mountain to its end at Davy
Brown Camp the canyon is filled with lush vegetation, cascading
pools and of course, tall firs trees—these called Big Cone Spruce.
This is the main trail leading from Figueroa Mountain down to the
Manzana Creek. A number of spur trails lead off it, making quite a
few different loop rides possible.

The Davy Brown Trail begins inauspiciously in a small
grass-covered saddle, but within a few hundred yards you will
find yourself immersed deep in the the narrow confines of Fir
Canyon, surrounded by Big Cone Spruce, large Kellogg oaks,
and Bigleaf maples. The trail itself provides intense single
track and you may want to walk some of it. But for those who
are technical experts, Davy Brown's trail will offer you Santa
Barbara's best single track.

A mile down the canyon the trail crosses to the right side of
the creek, then in a short distance back to the left. Below here
the riding is somewhat level and the canyon incredibly
beautiful.

At the next creek crossing you will find the memorial to
Edgar Davidson and shortly thereafter several connector
trails. The first is on the right and goes up to the Munch
Canyon Trail. A few yards below this you will find a connector

trail leading up and to the left. This leads to the Black Willow Springs Trail.

A half mile of more level canyon riding leads to the Roberts' ruins. Below here the trail passes through a layer of sandstone and then drops sharply again for several hundred yards. This is another section you may want to walk. The last mile of the ride again levels out and provides wonderful single track riding through the lush, green canyon to Davy Brown Campground.

At this point you have a choice of two return routes. The longer route is all on pavement and follows Sunset Valley to Cachuma Saddle and then up over Ranger Peak and back to the upper Davy Brown trailhead.

The more direct route is via the Figueroa Jeepway, which is located a .25 mile below the campground. To reach it, turn left on Sunset Valley Road, cross the creek, and ride to the large meadow with horse corrals. You will see the jeepway on the left. It goes across the meadow and up into a small canyon.

A few hundred yards up this is an intersection. The road continuing up the canyon is John Cody's road and eventually leads to the Sulphur Springs Trail. The Jeepway branches off to the left and rises steadily uphill for 4 miles to the Catway Turn left turn and ride up one short hill, then enjoy the downhill, which lasts for 2.5 miles until you reach Figueroa Mountain Road. Follow this to the left 1.7 miles back to the trailhead.

EAST PINERY LOOP

TRAIL INFORMATION: Distance—7 miles Elevation Loss—500'
to Munch Spur; 1100' elevation gain up to Ranger Saddle   Difficulty—Moderate with some technical riding

SANTA BARBARA RECREATIONAL MAP SERIES: Map #5—
Figueroa Mountain Hiking and Biking Routes—Trails #2 & 3

HIGHLIGHTS: This is one of the prettiest rides in Santa Barbara,
combining the beauty of Fir Canyon with a ride back up through an
aromatic grove of Yellow, Jeffrey, and Coulter pines. The canyon is
filled with lush vegetation, cascading pools and of course, tall firs
trees, while the route back combines some uphill single track and
an excellent graded dirt road that ends at the saddle at Ranger
Peak.

The first mile + of this ride is down Fir Canyon, a narrow
gorge cut through Monterey Shale and filled with spruce,
oaks, and maples. The single track is excellent though you
may want to walk some of it. When you reach the memorial to
Edgar Davidson, a bronze plaque set in a large serpentine
boulder, look for the Munch Spur Trail on the right side of the
creek.

The trail is steep for the first hundred yards. You will have
to push up this part, but after that the trail can be ridden. It
is slightly more than a half mile to the main Munch Canyon
Trail.

The connector trail ends at a dirt road. Turn right on this
and ride 50 yards up to the top of a saddle where you will find
an intersection. Straight ahead will lead you into Munch
Canyon. A left turn will take you down to Sunset Valley on an
old mining road. You want to make a right turn.

The right turn heads uphill and leads to the East Pinery. You will have to push for a short distance, but after this the balance of the route is composed of gentle switchbacks through an enchanting pine forest and can be ridden. The trail ends at the end loop at the bottom of the Pinery. From here it is 1.25 miles of easy uphill to Ranger Saddle. Turn right on the paved road and descend 2 miles on it to the Davy Brown trailhead.

MUNCH CANYON

TRAIL INFORMATION: Distance—11.8 miles   Elevation Loss—
1400' to Sunset Valley; 1400' gain back up over Ranger Saddle
Difficulty—Strenuous with some technical riding

SANTA BARBARA RECREATIONAL MAP SERIES: Map #5—
Figueroa Mountain Hiking and Biking Routes—Trails #2 & 6

HIGHLIGHTS: This ride combines the beauty of Fir Canyon with
the rugged chaparral of Munch Canyon, a combination of opposites
that is the trademark of the backcountry. Munch Canyon ends at
Sunset Valley where you can have a shuttle waiting for you or you
can turn right on the paved road and ride back to your car. An
alternative is to begin at Cachuma Saddle and get the steep riding
up to Ranger Saddle out of the way first. To avoid the technical
single track in Fir Canyon you can start at East Pinery and drop
down it to the Munch Canyon Trail.

The first mile + of this ride is down Fir Canyon, a narrow
gorge cut through Monterey Shale and filled with spruce,
oaks, and maples. The single track is excellent though you
may want to walk some of it. When you reach the memorial to
Edgar Davidson, a bronze plaque set in a large serpentine
boulder, look for the Munch Spur Trail on the right side of the
creek. The trail is steep the first hundred yards and you will
have to push up this part, but after that the trail can be ridden.

It is slightly more than a half mile to the main Munch
Canyon Trail. When the path ends at a dirt road, turn right on
this and ride 50 yards up to the top of a saddle where you will
find an intersection. To the right is the route to the East
Pinery. To the left is an old mining road which leads down to
Sunset Valley.

Straight ahead leads into Munch Canyon. The Munch Trail is fairly technical and overgrown in parts, but if you like single tracking, the route provides you with another way to enjoy an afternoon on the mountain. The first mile of the ride is down through the canyon. The trail is rocky and you may want to walk some sections. The last half leaves the canyon, turning to the left and crossing through the chaparral to intersect with the mining road. It is a half mile down to the Sunset Valley Road.

You can either turn left and drop down to the Figueroa Jeepway and take this back to your car or turn right and return on pavement. The climb is steady, 3.1 miles to Cachuma Saddle and then an even steeper 3.3 miles up to Ranger Saddle. Though a hard ride, it is beautiful in the later part of the day as the sun nears the horizon and hillsides glow in the light. From the saddle it is 2 miles of downhill back to the upper Davy Brown trailhead.

Ranger Peak

In the late 1890s when the US Topographical Survey Team began to work in this area, at first they wanted to name this peak after its first ranger, Edgar Davidson. The shy, retiring ranger had previously named it Alice Eastwood Peak in honor of the famous San Francisco botanist who had visited him at his station on a plant collecting trip (he had also named many of the other nearby geographical features such as Sunset Valley, Fir Canyon, the East Pinery, and Figueroa Mountain) and didn't want it named after him. Finally he suggested that the survey team call it Ranger Peak in honor of all rangers who had served the Forest Reserves. The name stuck.

If you have time, hike up the ridge just opposite the East Pinery Road to the top of the peak. The last hundred yards are pretty steep, but once on top you'll discover that it is flat and open, with views out over what seems like everything. It is a great place for lunch or just to relax for a few minutes. An afternoon here will be well spent.

DIRECTIONS: Ranger Peak can be accessed from either end of the Figueroa Mountain Loop. From Los Olivos, turn right on Figueroa Mountain Road (next to Mattei's tavern) and drive 16.5 miles. Ranger Peak is located at the high point on the loop road. A small turnout where you can park and a locked gate on the north side of the road marks Ranger Saddle and the road to the East Pinery. From the Santa Barbara side, turn right on Armour Ranch Road which is immediately after Highway 154 crosses the Santa Ynez River. Follow it a mile to Happy

Canyon, turn right and continue on this for slightly more than 10 miles to Cachuma Saddle (site of Forest Service Station). Turn left and drive uphill for 3.3 miles to Ranger Saddle.

The East Pinery Trails

Starting your rides on the East Pinery might be preferable if you would rather avoid some of the more technical single track riding found in Fir Canyon. You might also want to park at Cachuma Saddle and get the main uphill section from there to Ranger Saddle out of the way while your legs are still fresh.

Many more rides are available than those mentioned here, since the numerous trails and dirt roads offer endless combinations. As an example, for riders in top shape it is possible to descend East Pinery, take the Munch Spur to Fir Canyon, continue on down to Davy Brown, ascend the Jeepway to Catway Road, ride across this to Sulphur Springs Trail and then return via the Cody access road to Sunset Valley and back up this to Ranger Saddle, in all an energetic and super-gonzo 26 mile ride!

The rule on Figueroa Mountain is simple: be creative.

EAST PINERY LOOP

TRAIL INFORMATION: Distance—2.5 miles   Elevation Loss—
250' to end of loop   Difficulty—Easy, with no technical riding

HIGHLIGHTS: The route itself isn't long and it's actually not a trail
but a well graded road which goes down the main ridgeline leading
north from Ranger Peak. Yet it is an enchanting place; the ridge is
covered by tall Coulter pines and their ever-present smell. The
roads goes downhill gradually for 1.25 miles to the end of the ridge
where you can enjoy a fine picnic and wonderful views. Several
trails leading off this road provide access to other parts of the
mountain.

This easy ride is along an excellent dirt road which leads
down the north side of Ranger Peak, dropping 400' in elevation
to a loop at its end. Lush stands of Coulter pine, black oak, and
a low covering of manzanita provide excellent scenery and a
pleasant afternoon ride. In the Fall the numerous Kellogg
oaks in the area provide seasonal color. There are a host of
small niches to be found along the way, each providing a
picturesque and rustic picnic site, nicer than those found at
many of the established sites.

As you coast down the road you'll probably notice that most
of the trees are almost the same size. This is due to a forest fire
which burned through the area several decades ago. The
wildfire started in Davy Brown Campground and burned
unchecked up the north side of the mountain until stopped at
Figueroa Mountain Road. Most of the trees were actually
killed by the intense heat of the fire rather than the flames,
and afterwards most of them were cut down and hauled away.
The whole area was replanted after the salvage effort.

Though the trip to the end of East Pinery isn't long—only 1.25 miles—longer rides are possible by connecting with one of several trails leading off East Pinery into Munch, White Rock, and Fir canyons. To connect with the Munch Canyon spur, follow the East Pinery road to its end (a loop). Take the right fork of the loop for 100 yards, looking carefully for the trail which diagonals down and to the right. The gradual switchbacks through tall yellow pines are worth exploring even if you don't go all the way down to the Munch Canyon trail.

When you reach Munch Trail, you can continue down either into Fir or Munch canyons. Munch Trail leads immediately to the right. To get to Fir Canyon, turn left and ride 50 yards, and turn left again on the connector trail leading to it.

If you only want to ride out to the end of the Pinery loop, you can make it more strenuous by starting at Figueroa Camp, which adds 6 miles and an 800' climb, or at Cachuma Saddle, which adds 6 miles and a 1300' elevation gain.

WHITE ROCK TRAIL

TRAIL INFORMATION: Distance—6.5 miles   Elevation Loss—1600' to Sunset Valley Road; same elevation gain on the return trip Difficulty—Moderately strenuous with some technical riding on the White Rock Trail

SANTA BARBARA RECREATIONAL MAP SERIES: Map #5—Figueroa Mountain Hiking and Biking Routes—Trail #4

HIGHLIGHTS: The trail begins a quarter mile down the East Pinery, leading down to the right and along another pine-covered ridge to an old chrome mine, with all its equipment still in place. The beautiful white rock formation nearby is worthy of exploration though it isn't as easy as you might wish to get to it. The trail leads to Sunset Valley Road, a half mile below Cachuma Saddle.

White Rock Trail is named after the outcroppings of brilliant white sandstone a mile down the trail and just south of the historic chrome mine. This trail is the remnant of an old jeepway which once serviced the mine, though it is now overgrown enough to seem just a trail. It provides an enjoyable way to traverse from Ranger Peak to Sunset Valley Road below.

From the saddle near Ranger Peak follow East Pinery for .25 mile to the trailhead. Look carefully—it is easy to miss because it turns sharply back to the right. The route drops steeply downhill through loose Monterey Shale, across a pine-covered knoll, and then downhill again for a mile to a point where serpentine outcroppings mark the beginning of the mine tailings.

At the mine, which still has original wooden structures and camp remnants in place, the trail leads left for several hundred yards to a saddle (the Munch/Whiterock Connector Trail is located here) then turns sharply right and into Whiterock Canyon. A mile down the canyon, the trail crosses the creek goes over a saddle and follows a small creek for another .25 mile to its end at Sunset Valley Road.

From there it is .75 mile to Cachuma Saddle and 3.3 miles of steady uphill back to Ranger Saddle.

The Catway Road, a short distance before the turnoff to Zaca Peak.

The high point on the Catway Road provides great views of the San Rafael Wilderness. The Sierra Madre Mtns. are in the distance.

Catway Road

Catway Road begins 1 mile above the Figueroa Ranger Station and is an excellent and very smooth dirt road which cuts across the west flank of Figueroa Mountain following a prominent ridgeline for 8 miles to a deadend at Wildhorse overlook. The Catway offers excellent rides and, with the exception of several short, steep uphill sections, is gradual enough for all levels of riders.

The ridge route will provide you one of the most surprising excursions to be found in the Santa Barbara area. The road is smooth enough for those who only like to ride on pavement, yet primitive enough in feeling to give you a real taste of what the backcountry is all about.

For several miles the Catway undulates its way around the west edge of Figueroa Mountain. Then suddenly you come to the first of many saddles—or windows—through which you can look out and down on the San Rafael Wilderness. It is a special sight.

Around the corner the road turns left and from this point you follow the crest up and over a series of knolls (they are steep but not too long) which lead you closer and closer to Zaca Peak and farther and farther back into time.

There are plenty of picnic spots and places to enjoy the views, and if you feel like getting off your bike for a while, hikes to the Zaca Overlook, Zaca Lake, or down to the Manzana to soak in the creek or experience the pioneer homesteads.

One caution though—look out for motorcyclists who use the road. Though the Catway is legally off-limits to ORV use, many off-roaders who use the Jeepway, which is open to them, do venture out onto it.

DIRECTIONS: Turn right on Figueroa Mountain Road in Los Olivos (next to Mattei's tavern) and drive a little more than 12 miles to the Catway Road. Catway Road is an excellent and very smooth dirt road which cuts across the west flank of Figueroa Mountain following a prominent ridgeline for 8 miles to a deadend at Wildhorse overlook. It begins a mile above the Figueroa Ranger Station.

THE CATWAY

TRAIL INFORMATION: Distance—8 miles one way   Elevation Gain—800' to Zaca Peak; the road rises and falls along the way Difficulty—Moderate, though much easier if you ride only as far as the Zaca Peak turnoff

HIGHLIGHTS: The Catway Road provides a wonderful way to get a feeling for the backcountry. The road wanders through pine forests and steep, grass-covered hillsides for 8 miles. The first half is along the western slopes of Figueroa Mountain; the last half along a bony ridgeline leading to Zaca Peak. The views looking out over the San Rafael Wilderness are great.

For a short ride that ends with views over the entire San Rafael Wilderness, you can't beat the trip out to the Figueroa Jeepway and back. From Figueroa Mountain Road, the Catway rises gradually for 2.4 miles to the Black Willow Springs trailhead, gaining 550'. The saddle here provides the first views, with the Black Willow and Fir Canyon drainages directly below you and San Rafael Mountain in the far distance. From there it is just .3 mile to the Jeepway, and 180 degree views of the backcountry.

At this point the Catway turns to the left and follows the top of a long ridge that ends at Wildhorse Peak. From here on the riding is a bit more difficult as the road yo-yos up and over a series of knolls and peaks, several of which are fairly steep.

The steepest is a mile beyond the Jeepway. It is a half mile long but seems like forever. Just before the spur road to Zaca Peak, a second uphill awaits you, though it isn't as steep. The top of this ridge marks the high point along the Catway and from it you are looking directly down on Manzana Creek, the Castle Crags, and Hurricane Deck.

You are also looking almost directly into the Zaca Lake drainage. To see the lake you need to go a bit further. But this entails a long downhill ride which you will have to return back up later. Cedros Saddle is at the bottom of this 500' elevation drop. On one side of the saddle, the Zaca Trail leads down to the lake; on the other the Sulphur Springs Trail winds down into the Manzana drainage.

From Cedros Saddle it is an additional 1.75 miles to the Wildhorse overlook. There are more ups and downs, though the ride is scenic and provide more views of Zaca Lake, and at the end, a panorama of the lower Sisquoc River watershed.

To reach Zaca Lake, where you can enjoy a leisurely lunch before your trip back, take the trail from Cedros Saddle. It is 2 miles to the historic resort.

Other Rides

HELL'S HALF ACRE

TRAIL INFORMATION: Distance—5 miles one way; 9 miles to McKinley Saddle Elevation Gain—1300' to Hell's Half Acre; 2700' from Cachuma Saddle to McKinley Saddle; return trip is almost all downhill Difficulty—Moderately strenuous to very strenuous

SANTA BARBARA RECREATIONAL MAP SERIES: Map #5— Figueroa Mountain Hiking and Biking Routes—Trail #16

HIGHLIGHTS: Though the entire ride is along a dirt road, it provides views out over both the San Rafael Wilderness and the Santa Ynez Valley. The road follows a long ridgeline that leads to the wilderness's namesake—San Rafael Peak, which is 6593' in elevation. In the winter months when it is clear, you can see the snow-capped Sierras from the ridge. The ultimate adventure is to ride to McKinley Saddle and from there hike the remaining 2 miles to the top of San Rafael Peak.

DIRECTIONS: Turn right on Armour Ranch Road, which is immediately after Highway 154 crosses the Santa Ynez River. Follow it a mile to Happy Canyon, turn right and continue on this for slightly more than 10 miles to Cachuma Saddle (site of Forest Service Station). The route to Hell's Half Acre follows a dirt road starting from the east side of the saddle.

On the surface, Hell's Half Acre doesn't exactly sound like the kind of place you'd ordinarily go out of your way to visit. But the road you ride along winds up the long ridge to San Rafael Peak and on either side of it you have lots of great views. The road isn't too steep and is well graded, which means you can spend more time concentrating on the views and less time watching what your front wheel might be about to hit.

As you reach Cachuma Saddle, look for a large parking area opposite the ranger station. The route begins on the east side

From there it is an easy .5 mile of gentle uphill to the road's end on the south face of Zaca Peak. The Overlook Mountain Trail begins here, providing a pleasant break before the return ride back to your car. The trail leads a quarter mile down to another saddle where the overgrown section begins. Look for an opening in the manzanita and after a few hundred yards this opens enough that the hiking is fairly easy. The rest of the route follows a long ridgeline through pine forests, with views now and then down on the lake.

ZACA LAKE LOOP

TRAIL INFORMATION: Distance—34.6 miles Elevation Gain—
3500' Difficulty—Strenuous for the full loop; shorter more
moderate options are possible

HIGHLIGHTS: Though this is a long ride, it is absolutely the best
you'll find anywhere in Santa Barbara County. The ride follows
Figueroa Mountain Road to the Catway and then continues along
it to a trail leading down to Zaca Lake. You have the beauty of the
Santa Ynez Valley, the rolling grass and pine-covered hills leading
to Figueroa Mountain, and awesome views of the backcountry from
the Catway on the first half of the ride and the solitude of Zaca Lake
(you have lunch at the lodge there), the enchanting grace of Foxen
Canyon, and perhaps a stop at the Firestone Vineyard on the second
half. Dinner at Mattei's Tavern will top off the day.

From Mattei's Tavern the first 5 miles of this spectacular
loop ride is across the valley plain and eventually up through
the lower part of the Birabent Creek watershed. You'll find
country ranches, a scattering of homes, acres and acres of
pasture land, and Midland School along the way. Near the
upper end of the drainage, the road crosses a small bridge, and
from there the work begins.

The next mile takes you sharply up and onto a long, broad
ridge that leads to Figueroa Mountain. The hills are a combination of open grassland, oak groves, digger pines, and
outcroppings of serpentine that give the landscape an overall
feeling of greenness, even in the summer when the grass is
golden yellow. The uphill seems to continue forever, each time
you look at the pine-topped mound of Figueroa Mountain you
wonder if it is getting any closer.

But just as you are firmly convinced that you will never get there, the Figueroa Mountain Guard Station comes into view and just beyond that you come to Sawmill Basin, and finally, the Catway. The turn onto the Catway brings you into a different world. The rolling hills are left behind and now you are totally immersed by pine trees.

The road is dirt, but it is smooth enough that you don't have to focus on it. Rather, you can just settle into a low gear, an easy pace, and enjoy the beauty and smells that surround you. The uphill is steady though not too steep for 2.5 miles, then almost without warning you come to a window formed by a saddle between two hills and have your first look out on the backcountry. It is impressive.

From here the Catway turns to the left, heading directly west on a long, thin ridge, with plenty of short uphills, and several downhills to keep you occupied. Four miles of this, along with more backcountry vistas, pine forests, and happy riding bring you to Cedros Saddle, which is at the end of a long downhill.

The trail to the lake leads left on a path that twists through an oak and pine forest for a short distance, then begins to drop sharply downhill. Depending on your single track abilities you may want to walk some of this, but otherwise the riding is great for the next two miles. Near the bottom the trail levels and then widens into a dirt road that passes through a picnic and camping area, lots more oak groves and meadows, and a half mile later, opens onto the lake.

Though only a few hundred yards in diameter, Zaca Lake glitters like a precious jewel in this sylvan setting. A small road circles it, and in small niches, there are picnic tables and places to sit and relax. On the far side there is a small dock, open deck area, and ranch style resort, all that seems perfectly suited to this setting. And for a lunch spot.

The road out leads down the valley, and for the first half mile the riding is level. Then suddenly it drops out of sight, and for the next mile you glide downhill through switchback after switchback, causing you to lose more than 700 feet in elevation, and making you realize just how high up in the mountains the lake is actually located.

At the bottom of the drop the road levels, becoming a serpentine path that wanders back and forth down the creek before opening in a mile more of riding to farmland and cattle grazing in the fields. This section is the only part of the ride which has an obvious disadvantage—because the road is dirt and the lake somewhat popular, you may be "dusted" by the cars which pass you. Fortunately, the paved road is less than 15 minutes from here.

Just beyond the closed gate at the entrance to Zaca Lake is Foxen Canyon Road. Though paved, it is narrow and has a very country feeling to it. Two miles of riding down it bring you to a left turn (Foxen Canyon Road goes left here) and the last uphill. But there is a solution at hand. Rather than tackling it immediately, the Firestone Vineyard is just a bit further down the road. There is a small picnic area there, but the real attraction is the opportunity to join the winery tour and sample some of their award winning wines.

After enjoying this detour, retrace your route the few hundred yards back to the Foxen Canyon turn, go over that last hill, and then enjoy the last few miles of level riding you have left that take you back to Mattei's Tavern. If you've been really smart, you've already made arrangements for dinner there.

NOTE: A shorter version of this ride, 21 miles in length, can be made by leaving a car at Mattei's and driving up to the Catway with your bikes and then driving back up for this vehicle after the ride is over.

CATWAY/CODY LOOP

TRAIL INFORMATION: Distance—19.25 miles for the full loop; 14 for the shorter Jeepway Loop Elevation Gain—2500' Difficulty—Strenuous; less so if you drive up the Catway to the Jeepway and begin from there

HIGHLIGHTS: This ride provides backcountry views and pine-covered hills from the Catway, a short section of single track on the Sulphur Springs Trail, and a longer section of dirt road back to the Davy Brown area. The ride back up the Jeepway is steep.

The Catway/Cody loop is one of the more strenuous rides available in this area, but it provides you with a lot of the best of this country—great backcountry views, a ride through pine forests, single track riding, and the feeling of being deep inside very wild country.

Begin this ride from the intersection of Figueroa Mountain Road and the Catway, or if you want to make it a bit shorter, drive up the Catway to the Figueroa Jeepway (2.8 miles) and start from there. Continue along the Catway on your bike until you reach Cedros Saddle which is at the end of a long downhill and is marked by a wooden sign. The trail to Zaca Lake leads off the left side of the saddle and opposite it, on the right, you'll find the Sulphur Springs Trail.

The trail drops for a mile down to a dirt road. This is an access road that leads down to the Manzana to an inholding in the San Rafael Wilderness owned by world famous sculptor John Cody. If you would like to see his works, they are on display at the Cody Gallery in Los Olivos. The lower road and Manzana Creek are in wilderness and are off limits to mountain bikes. Please do not go down the road (it's a 1000' elevation drop to the river and a long, long climb out, even on foot).

Follow the Cody road to the right, winding around Mill and Coldwater Creek drainages for 6 miles to Sunset Valley Road a half mile below Davy Brown Campground. This part of the ride is somewhat frustrating, especially if you aren't in good shape. As you cross each of the drainages you climb up over the ridges separating them, and then drop back down. On the final ridge, before you drop down into Sunset Valley, you can see the top of the Jeepway not too far above you. But to get there you must ride down to the lower end of it (an 800' elevation loss) and then regain this on the way up.

The Jeepway veers off to the right a few hundred yards before you get to Sunset Valley. You'll know you are near it when you get to the locked gate at the bottom of Cody's road.

The climb up to the top of the Catway is 4 miles and 2000' in elevation gain. At the end of the day, with tired legs, this is definitely the hardest part of the ride. But you do have a nice treat waiting for you—an exhilarating and much deserved 2.5 mile downhill to Figueroa Mountain Road.

NOTE: if you are camping at Davy Brown, you can begin this ride by going up the Jeepway first when your legs are ready for it, and having the less difficult climbs at the end of your ride.

BLACK WILLOW SPRINGS

TRAIL INFORMATION: Distance—10.5 miles Elevation Loss—
1100' from Catway to Fir Canyon; 1100' gain up to Ranger Saddle
Difficulty—Moderately strenuous

SANTA BARBARA RECREATIONAL MAP SERIES: Map #5—
Figueroa Mountain Hiking and Biking Routes—Trail #8

HIGHLIGHTS: Though not a long trail, Black Willow Springs
provides not only a beautiful route from the Catway into Fir
Canyon, but a sense of solitude that belies the fact that it is so close
to established roads and camps. You can either continue down Fir
Canyon or go up the Munch Connector to the East Pinery.

DIRECTIONS: From Figueroa Mountain Road drive 2.4 miles up
the Catway to a small saddle which provides your first view out into
the San Rafael Wilderness. The trail begins here, though it is a bit
difficult to spot due to an accumulation of grass.

I can't remember exactly where I was, but one day I looked
over at the far side of Figueroa Mountain and I could see the
upper end of this trail switching back and forth through a
steep section of golden yellow grass. My curiosity was sparked.
Where did it lead, I wondered?

Later, on another day I was resting at a saddle along the
Catway Road, having mountain biked up from the valley.
While I was sitting there I remembered that earlier trip. I
started looking around for a trail, and there it was! To my
chagrin, the place where I was relaxing turned out to be the top
of it. The first switchback was a bit overgrown, but after that
the trail was easy to follow. I couldn't believe it. Now I use it
regularly.

Several short switchbacks lead down the steep grassy slope and then the trail turns to the right, cutting across the lower part of Figueroa Mountain. The trail drops 600' meandering through tall big cone spruce for 1 mile to Willow Springs, a secluded glen more reminiscent of Oregon.

You'll probably want to walk your bike at first. There are only a few switchbacks and below these the trail can be ridden. Most of the section above Willow Springs is relatively straight, with a slight curve to the left as it follows the bowl-shaped northern slope of Figueroa Mountain through ample amounts of Big Cone Spruce.

There isn't any springs that are recognizable. What you will find is a small creek deep in shade, and lots of trees. The Black Willow Springs Trail follows the creek downstream. The start of it is hard to find but once on it you won't have any trouble following it. I wouldn't recommend it, however, unless you love riding through poison oak thickets, with an occasional one slapping you in the face.

What seems to be the main trail leads east, straight across the creek and uphill. This is actually a connector which leads to the upper part of Fir Canyon and is the preferred route. Just to the left of the hill look for a series of sandstone outcroppings. They are fun to explore. It is a mile to Fir Canyon on this trail. Most of it is good single track, though when I was last there, a small oak was across the path, necessitating a bit of maneuvering to get through.

When you reach Fir Canyon, head upstream. The Munch Spur is just a hundred yards upstream. Follow this to the Munch intersection (see Fir Canyon trail descriptions), turn right and continue up to East Pinery and from there to to Ranger Saddle. The ride back along Figueroa Mountain Road to the Catway is 3.7 miles of mostly downhill.

ZACA PEAK OVERLOOK

TRAIL INFORMATION: Distance— 6.2 miles   Elevation Gain—
800' to Zaca Peak; the road rises and falls along the way   Difficulty—
Moderate

HIGHLIGHTS: The Catway Road provides a wonderful way to get
a feeling for the backcountry. The road wanders through pine
forests and steep, grass-covered hillsides for 8 miles. Slightly less
than 5 miles along it, a spur road leads for a mile and a half out to
Zaca Peak, where you have views of the lake and the entire Santa
Ynez Valley.

Whenever I'm out on the Catway, I always try to leave
enough time to ride out to the overlook because it is a pretty
ride and the views are great. Plus, I love the short (though
overgrown) hike out towards Overlook Mountain.

The ride across the Catway is 4.7 miles to the Zaca Peak
turnoff, which you need to look for carefully because it is easy
to miss. The spur comes in on a diagonal from the left just as
the Catway begins the long descent to Cedros Saddle.

The Zaca road drops down for .25 mile, then rises over a
small knoll and then drops a bit more sharply for .75 miles to
a saddle. If you keep your eyes focused on the left side of the
road as you coast downhill you should be able to spot the upper
end of the La Jolla Trail.

The first mile down this trail winds through a canopy of tall
pine trees and makes a very pleasant side hike. I rode this back
to my car once—and only once. The ride down into Birabent
Canyon is spectacular single tracking, but at the bottom you
face over 2 miles of pushing, first through the upper end of the
canyon (which is really pretty) and then up a mile of switchbacks
which is no fun at all.

of the saddle. The first mile is the steepest as it curves around the west and north sides of a tall, pointed mountain known as Cachuma Peak. This area offers the first views out over the San Rafael Wilderness. The next 1.5 miles beyond this are only slightly uphill and continue to provide an overview of the entire wilderness.

At the 3 mile point the road cuts through a saddle on the east side of Cachuma Mountain and you shift from vistas of the backcountry to views out over the Santa Ynez Valley and the Channel Islands. The next 2 miles to Hell's Half Acre are almost level. In actuality the flat meadow is probably more like Hell's Twenty Acres—for it is much larger in size than its name would indicate. And the views are certainly not like those from Hell.

To the north you are looking directly down on Manzana Narrows and over the sandstone ledges that form the eastern edge of Hurricane Deck. On the south horizon, the Channel Islands shimmer on the horizon, looking far larger than they really are.

Continuing beyond this open meadow turns the ride from being relatively moderate to a hard core adventure. The road drops slightly down to a saddle and across the back side of a hill which still has the charred remains of hundreds of Big Cone Spruce on it. This area burned in 1966 when an airplane crash caused the Wellman Fire.

East of this the "section from hell" begins at the base of a series of impressive sandstone cliffs that lead up onto McKinley Mountain. The road is steep, loose and almost impossible to ride. The worst part of it is that you can see all of this part of the road from Hell's Half Acre, meaning that you know exactly how bad it will be before you ever get there. Plan on pushing for most of a half mile or more.

Eventually you do get to a more level stretch on the back side of McKinley Mountain, though there are just enough short little hills to keep your legs from fully recovering. McKinley Springs is a small camp located at the 7 mile point. There is a small table there and may be water, though you can't count on it. The saddle is an additional 2 miles. It is a round, flat open dirt area, with not much to recommend it other than you can climb to the top of either McKinley or San Rafael mountains from there.

The 6,200 foot crest of San Rafael is 2 miles but I recommend it highly. Though it is chaparral covered, the view from there is absolutely spectacular, and a short walk to the east of the peak brings you to the start of the Mission Pines and several square miles of the most enchanting sandstone and pine hideaways you will ever find. An incredibly wonderful camp— Mission Pine Springs—is 2 more miles down into this primeval wonderland.

I try to do this ride when I know there will be a full moon. The road is open and wide enough you almost don't even need a light and this makes it possible for you to spend the entire day up on top.

FIGUEROA LOOKOUT

TRAIL INFORMATION: Distance—2.5 miles one way   Elevation Gain—500' Difficulty—Moderate

HIGHLIGHTS: Though not a long ride this leads to the top of Figueroa Mountain and from its 4,500 foot crest you can see everywhere. There is a small picnic area at the overlook and also at Pino Alto, where you will find a short self-guided nature trail. You have Coulter pines on either side of you all the way up. You can extend the ride by starting at Sawmill Basin.

DIRECTIONS: Though the spur road leading to the top of Figueroa Mountain can be accessed from either end of the Figueroa Mountain Loop, the shortest route there is from the Los Olivos end. When you reach Los Olivos, turn north on Figueroa Mountain Road (next to Mattei's tavern). It is 13.5 miles to the spur road, which is a half mile before you reach Figueroa Campground. The turnoff is well marked and there is ample parking near it.

If you want to choose one ride to do in the spring, say sometime between late March and the end of April, this is the one to do. When the California poppies turn fluorescent orange, the bush lupine open their lilac colored blossoms, filling the air with a pungent aroma, and scores of other wildflowers carpet the upper slopes of Figueroa Mountain, this place becomes Alice's Wonderland.

My personal recommendation would be to start at Sawmill Basin. The countryside there is almost flat and this is where the floral display begins in ernest. From this point it is just a half mile to the Catway Road and about the same distance more on Figueroa Mountain Road to the spur route to the overlook.

The road is moderately steep, rising 1000', the grade is relatively even so the uphill is spread throughout the entire 2.5 miles. The first half of the road winds around the east side of Figueroa Mountain through almost solid Coulter pine forests. It then turns sharply back to the west as it goes around to the back side of the mountain. The forests are equally thick and views of the Santa Ynez Valley are replaced by those of the backcountry.

Two miles from the start of the spur road a turnout to the left leads to Pino Alto, a Sierra-like picnic area that has interpretive information as well as a short self-guided nature trail. The Figueroa Mountain Overlook is an additional .5 mile on the main spur. Shortly up this you will notice a road that leads diagonally off to the left. This goes to other picnic sites. Above this turnoff the pine trees seem to fade away and the top of the mountain is almost all open grasslands and wildflowers. The lookout can be seen from here. Once it was manned 24 hours a day during fire season, though today it is a relic of the past.

What can I say about the view from the top? Nothing really. It is too much for words. You will just have to experience it for yourself.

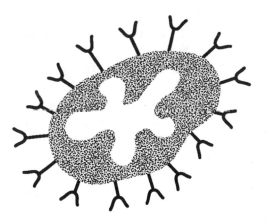

FISH CREEK SPUR

TRAIL INFORMATION: Distance—3.5 miles   Elevation Loss/Gain—300' Difficulty—Moderately easy

SANTA BARBARA RECREATIONAL MAP SERIES: Map #5—Figueroa Mountain Hiking and Biking Routes—Trail #7

HIGHLIGHTS: This is just a spur trail leading from Fish Creek down into Sunset Valley but is a ride if you are also picnicking in the oak filled valley. A dirt road leads through the southeastern part of Sunset Valley to the spur trail. It can be combined with a hike down into the Fish Creek drainage.

The upper end of the spur trail begins 1.7 miles down from Cachuma Saddle on the left side of the road just before it drops down into Sunset Valley. The lower end is in Sunset Valley, 3.1 miles from the Saddle.

The easiest way to ride this loop is by riding up the paved road and then dropping back down into Sunset Valley on the trail. It is 1.5 miles on the pavement to the upper trailhead. The first half of the ride is level as you pedal through the valley, with the uphill mostly in the last quarter mile.

If you'd like to combine a short hike with the ride, stash your bikes and walk down into the Fish Creek drainage. There is no real trail (the cow trails are pretty good) but three-quarters of a mile down the drainage you will discover a delightful pool, as well as a series of cascades.

On the return trip look for the trail on the left side of the road. It is pretty easy to spot. The first half mile of it cuts across a chaparral-covered hillside. Then it drops down into Sunset Valley where the trail becomes a wide path that meanders through a lush oak forest.

Author, enjoying a last glimpse of the San Rafael Wilderness from the crest of the Catway Road. Views like this are typical in this area.

Mountain Bike Trail Volunteers

Mountain Bike Trail Volunteers was formed in 1989 for the purpose of organizing mountain bikers to do trail maintenance. It was felt that this would help counteract some of the "bad press" associated with our sport and help the trails at the same time. Since then, MBTV has also been involved in local land access issues and is trying to provide mountain biker education and awareness of concerns raised by hikers and equestrian groups.

By helping the MBTV you can have an impact in dealing with any or all of the above. MBTV recognizes the need to demonstrate that a large number of mountain bikers care about the condition of our local trails and the safety of those who use them.

Local mountain bikers need to show the Forest Service, hikers, and equestrian groups that there are a large number of bicyclists in our area who will work to help make the trails safe and enjoyable for all users. Your name on the MBTV list will help. If you feel you can spare it, a donation will also help.

Of course, volunteering not only helps keep trails open and in the best possible condition, but is also rewarding and sometimes, fun. Helping the Mountain Bike Trail Volunteers doesn't just mean working on trails. Other ways you can help include attending meetings, doing research, writing letters, and contacting government officials concerning trail issues.

Perhaps the most important thing, other than trail maintenance, you can assist with is helping to train and educate mountain bikers on the safest and most environmentally sensitive ways to use our local trails.

Count Me In!
I Want To Keep The Trails Open To
Mountain Bikers

For Further Information Contact Steve Silva
225 Valdez Avenue Goleta, CA 93117
(805) 683-0371 or 967-1313

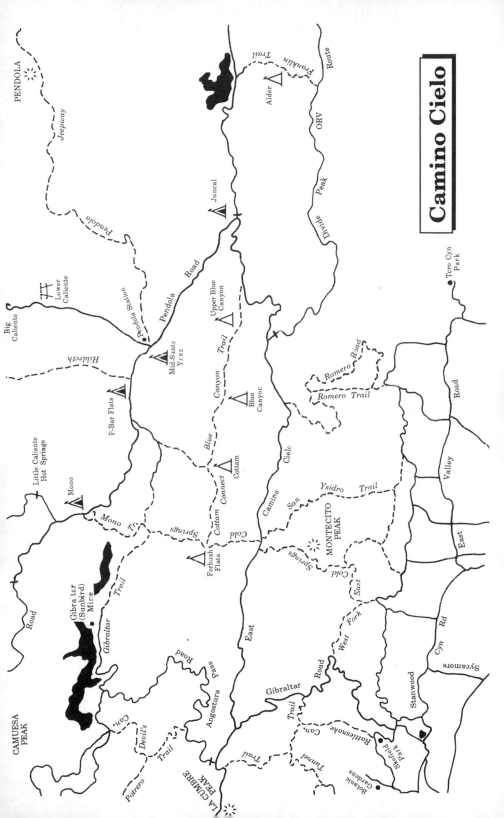

Camino Cielo

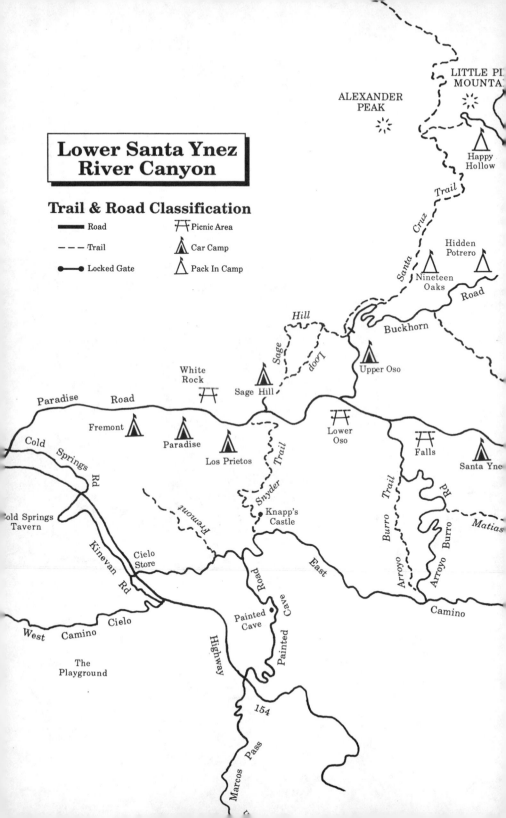

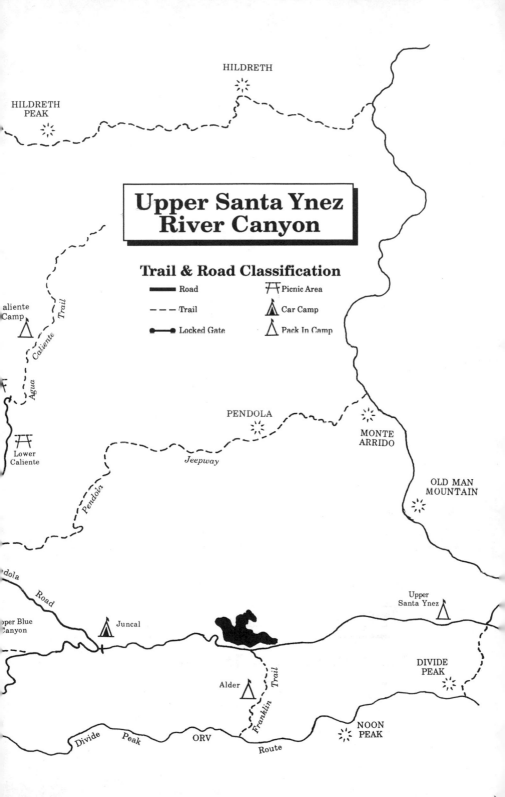

HILDRETH

HILDRETH
PEAK

Upper Santa Ynez
River Canyon

Trail & Road Classification

▬▬▬ Road	🏕 Picnic Area
– – – Trail	⛺ Car Camp
●━● Locked Gate	⛺ Pack In Camp

aliente
Camp

Caliente Trail

Agua

🏕
Lower
Caliente

PENDOLA

MONTE
ARRIDO

OLD MAN
MOUNTAIN

Jeepway

Pendola

dola

Road

per Blue
anyon

⛺ Juncal

Upper
Santa Ynez ⛺

DIVIDE
PEAK

Alder ⛺

Franklin Trail

NOON
PEAK

Divide Peak   ORV

Route

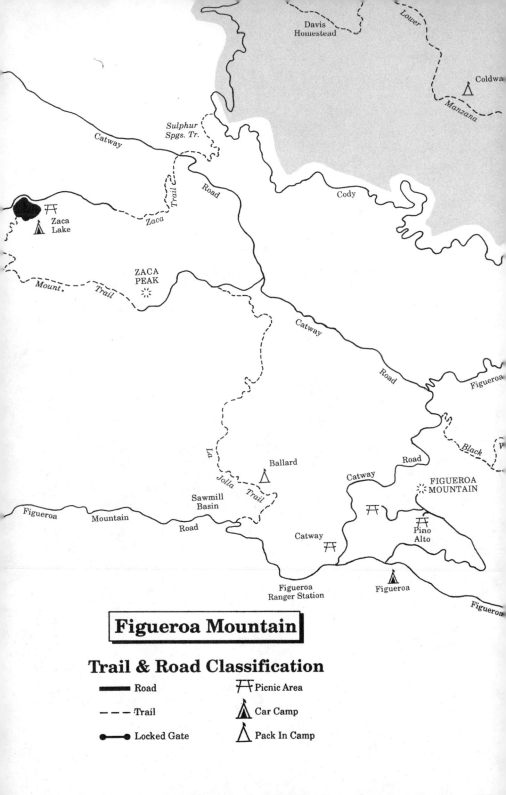

Davis
Homestead

Lower

Coldwa

Manzana

Catway

Sulphur
Spgs. Tr.

Road

Cody

Zaca
Lake

Zaca

Trail

Mount .

Trail

ZACA
PEAK

Catway

Road

Figueroa

Black

La

Jolla

Ballard

Sawmill
Basin

Trail

Road

Catway

Catway

FIGUEROA
MOUNTAIN

Road

Figueroa

Mountain

Road

Catway

Pino
Alto

Figueroa
Ranger Station

Figueroa

Figueroa

Figueroa Mountain

Trail & Road Classification

▬▬▬ Road   ⛩ Picnic Area

– – – Trail   ▲ Car Camp

●—● Locked Gate   △ Pack In Camp

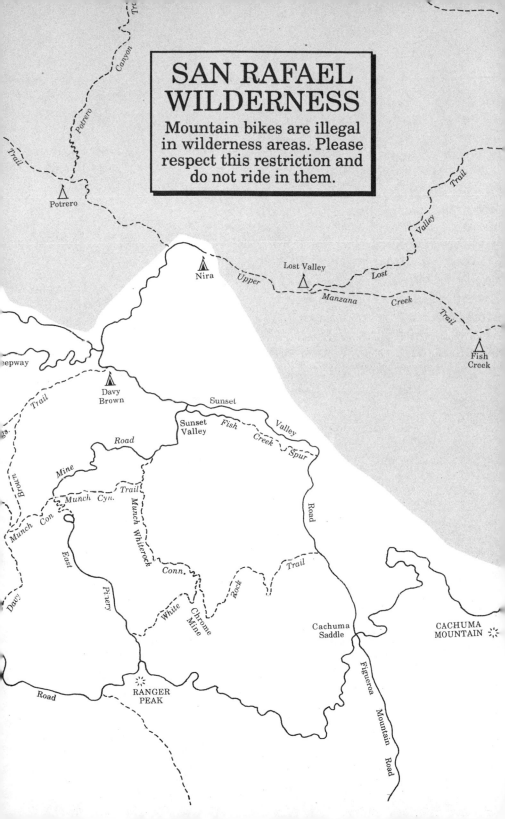